Rug Tufting

Guillaume Neves
@atelierpaolo

STACKPOLE
BOOKS
Essex, Connecticut
Blue Ridge Summit, Pennsylvania

STACKPOLE BOOKS
An imprint of Globe Pequot, the trade division of
The Rowman & Littlefield Publishing Group, Inc.
4501 Forbes Blvd., Ste. 200
Lanham, MD 20706
www.rowman.com

Distributed by NATIONAL BOOK NETWORK
800-462-6420

Original French title: Tufting
© 2022 Ėditions Eyrolles, Paris France

Graphic design and layout: Marthe Oréal | SMARTHE
Pages 64, 70, 82, 94, 104, 114, 124, and 138: photos of the creations and styling are from Sabine Mérillon (@miss_etc on Instagram). Page 46: Heiko Küverling/iStock/Getty Images Plus via Getty Images. Page 160: Domestika (domestika.org). All other photos and templates are by the author.

All rights reserved. No part of this book may be reproduced in any form or by any electronic or mechanical means, including information storage and retrieval systems, without written permission from the publisher, except by a reviewer who may quote passages in a review.

The contents of this book are for personal use only. Patterns herein may be reproduced in limited quantities for such use. Any large-scale commercial reproduction is prohibited without the written consent of the publisher.

We have made every effort to ensure the accuracy and completeness of these instructions. We cannot, however, be responsible for human error, typographical mistakes, or variations in individual work.

British Library Cataloguing in Publication Information available

Library of Congress Cataloging-in-Publication Data available
ISBN 978-0-8117-7574-8 (paper : alk. paper)
ISBN 978-0-8117-7595-3 (electronic)

∞™ The paper used in this publication meets the minimum requirements of American National Standard for Information Sciences—Permanence of Paper for Printed Library Materials, ANSI/NISO Z39.48-1992.

Foreword

After studying communications in Bordeaux, I had the opportunity to manage a restaurant. Then, when I was 22, I opened my own bakery. At the time, I had a blog that really helped me to become more-known. A year later, I moved to Paris, where I worked in chocolate, leather goods, and fashion. I held various positions, from salesperson to marketing manager. These incredible experiences allowed me to engage in many different things.

I'm very curious by nature and have always loved learning new things—it's what drives me! In my spare time, I like to draw and am fascinated by symbols and what they can mean to each of us, as well as by Mediterranean images and the retro world of the 1960s and 1970s.

In 2019, I set out to find a rug for my home. I was looking for something out of the ordinary, responsibly made, and reasonably priced. After much research, I concluded that the rug of my dreams did not exist. I had to make it myself! That's how I came across tufting. It's a very interesting craft for those who love drawing and textiles and want to transform their work into everyday objects. At the time, this technique was still unknown to the general public, and only major manufacturers had the appropriate machinery and equipment. With a bit of luck, I found my first gun, unearthed some tufting cloth, and learned how to build my first frame. And off I went!

My first attempt was a disaster! A rug that I intended to be rectangular turned out to be a trapezoid, full of holes. It was enough to discourage me, but I couldn't let it go to waste! After all, I wanted my ideal rug! So, I took the time to really learn how to use the gun, to adjust my speed, and to find the right amount of yarn, as well as how to perfect the finishing steps so the end product would be as neat and polished as possible. This is how Atelier Paolo was born, a way to offer unique, handcrafted pieces.

But why "Paolo"? I wanted a name with a sunny ring to it, one that smacked of summer vacations and brought back memories of my grandparents' home in Portugal.

Today, I'm lucky enough to collaborate with artists and brands, sell my pieces all over the world, as well as offer introductory workshops and an online course (on the Domestika platform). For me, writing this book is the culmination of everything I've learned about this technique and an opportunity to pass on my knowledge of tufting. It is aimed at all those who wish to create original pieces for their interiors, or who want to start selling tufted creations.

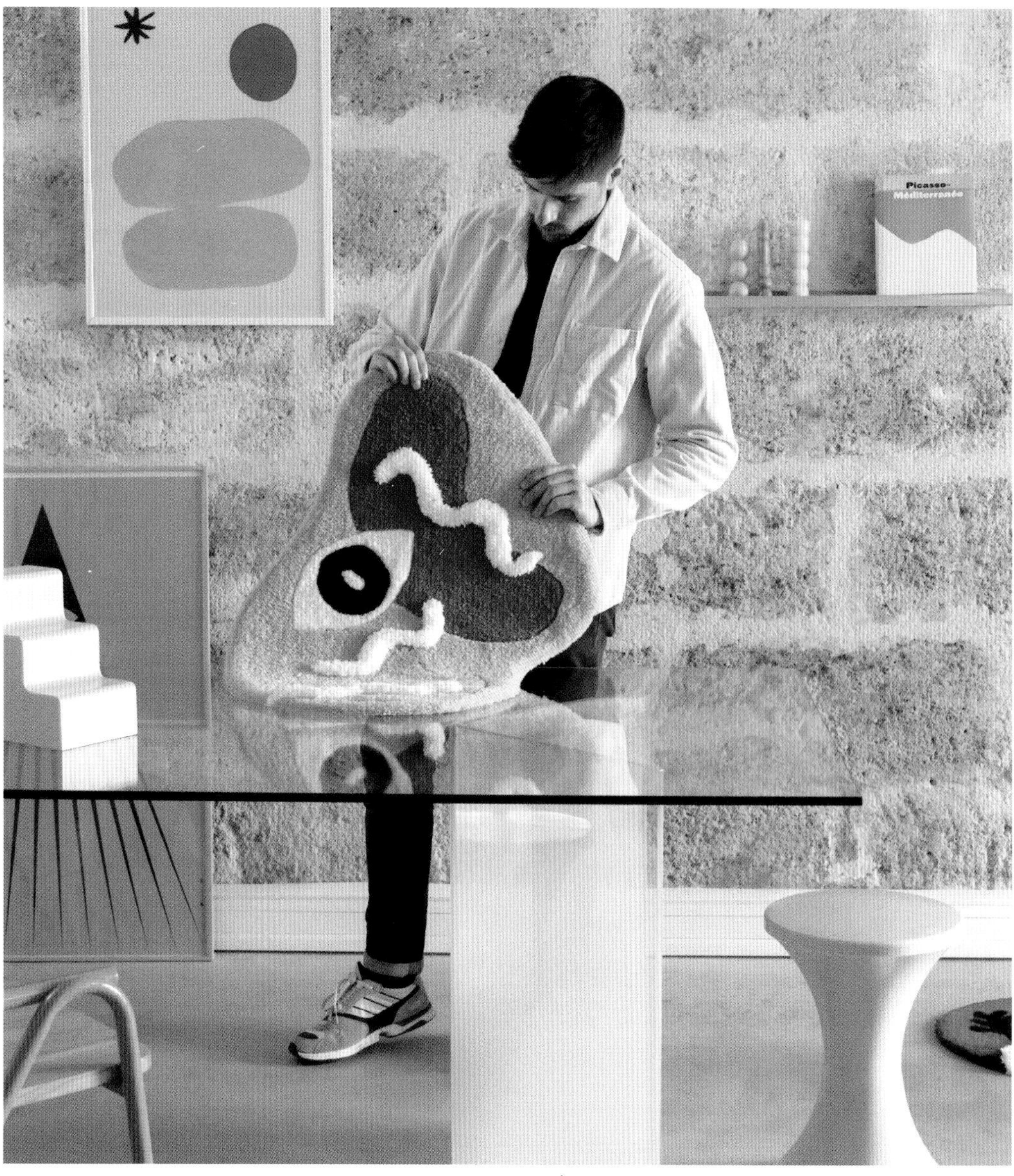

CONTENTS

Technical Guide

Tufting requires an investment in a few tools and materials to make the job easier. Starter kits are available from specialist retailers for around $400 to $500. That's about the cost of the initial investment you'll need to start tufting!

Tufting Gun

The first investment you'll need to make to get started is a tufting gun. This is used to insert yarn at a high speed onto a stretched cloth.

There are two commercially available models: cut pile and loop pile. A good tufting gun costs around $250 to $300.

Tufter's Checklist

The Essentials

- Tufting gun and lubricant for micromechanisms
- A tufting frame
- Special tufting cloth
- Heavy backing fabric
- Balls of yarn
- Rug binding tape
- Glue for carpet and flexible flooring
- Scissors, various sizes: a large pair of heavy-duty fabric scissors, a small pair for finishing and, optionally, duckbill or applique scissors for trimming
- A large ruler
- Fabric felt-tip pen or large black marker (Sharpie-type)
- Trowel
- Spatula, putty knife, or disposable vinyl gloves
- Flat brush, ½ in. (1.5 cm) wide
- Pet clippers
- Wire brush
- Ball winder
- Tweezers
- Needle threader
- Vacuum cleaner

Optional but Very Practical

- Manual carpet shaver
- Wooden compass
- Overhead projector or video projector
- Masking tape

Equipment for Safe Tufting

- Noise-cancelling headphones
- Safety goggles
- Worksite protective mask

- With the loop pile model, the yarn is inserted into the fabric without cutting it—forming a loop. This method is similar to the punch needle. This gun has no internal scissors. Each line of yarn produced must therefore be cut manually before pulling out the gun.

- With the cut model, scissors cut the yarn at high speed. The work has a thick, shaggy appearance.

Personally, I only use the cut pile model, as I find it looks more aesthetically pleasing. But it's all a matter of taste! If I want a curly look on small parts, I prefer the punch needle.

The most common guns are the ***AK-I (cut pile)*** and ***AK-II (loop pile)***, which generally have blue handles. They can be used to tuft different heights (from ¼ to ¾ in. [7 to 18 mm] for the cut pile, from ⅛ to ½ in. [4 to 13 mm] for the loop). To change the size, follow the instructions supplied with the gun or the step-by-step instructions on the Tuftinglove YouTube channel.

The AK-1N gun is a true 2-in-1 (loop pile and cut pile), offering both methods. To switch from one to the other, you must dismantle several mechanisms to change needles. This operation is a little tedious at first but becomes easier with a little practice. This gun costs around $200.

If you intend to use both methods regularly, I'd advise you to invest in two separate machines for greater comfort and to avoid dismantling the gun each time you change methods.

Whichever gun you choose, you'll need to clean and lubricate its more delicate parts before each use (page 38). A 3-in-1 multipurpose oil for micromechanisms is ideal.

Where to Buy a Tufting Gun

Except on the Internet, where the tufting market is mainly concentrated, it's very difficult to find a place that sells tufting guns. There are numerous e-commerce stores or platforms offering models at all prices, as well as all the other tools and materials you need to get started.

I strongly advise against buying from the huge platforms like Amazon or AliExpress, even if the prices offered are more attractive. Your gun is a complex machine with many mechanisms, so you need to be able to rely on quality after-sales service in the event of a problem. Only specialized sites will be able to respond quickly to your problems.

Here's a list of my favorite sites for worry-free ordering (worldwide delivery).

United States: tuftinggun.com tuft-love.com
France: letufting.fr
Belgium: tufting-stuff.shop
Spain: tuftingaddicts.com
Netherlands: tuftingshop.com tuftingeurope.com etsy.com/fr/shop/Tuftopia
Switzerland: tuftinglove.com
Australia: australiantuftingsupplies.com tuftcity.com

Primary Tufting Cloth

Primary tufting cloth is the support on which to tuft and make incredible creations! Be careful not to choose just any fabric. If it is not suitable for this technique, you risk making a hole in it and damaging your gun.

I recommend special tufting fabric. Created specifically for tufting, it is very sturdy. It features an open even-weave structure with rows of small holes that allow the gun's needle to insert the yarn, as well as woven marking lines that serve as reference points for stretching it onto the frame. It is available in two colors.

- **Gray cloth**, marked every 19 in. (50 cm), is generally 100% polyester. I recommend this type for larger pieces, as this material is more durable and better withstands the gun's tension.
- **White cloth**, marked every 2 in. (5 cm), is a cotton-polyester blend. This is a better choice for small- and medium-sized tufted items.

For a more natural alternative, opt for **burlap**. This backup solution has a drawback, however: it doesn't do well with tension, tears easily, and is less supple than special tufting fabric. It should be avoided if you wish to create medium- to large-sized pieces.

FROM LEFT TO RIGHT: GRAY CLOTH, WHITE CLOTH, AND BURLAP

Below is a table comparing the different types of fabric available.

Type of Fabric	Special Gray Tufting Cloth	Special White Tufting Cloth	Burlap
Composition	100% polyester	35% cotton 65% polyester blend	100% burlap
Advantages	Ideal when making large items	Reference lines every 2 in. (5 cm) for even stretching	Best alternative if you can't find special tufting fabric
Disadvantages	None	With white or light yarn, mistakes are harder to see on the fabric	Tears easily as it is less supple. Use for making small pieces only.
Budget	About $11 per sq. yd. (m)	About $11 per sq. yd. (m)	About $3 per sq. yd. (m)
Where can I find it?	Online stores	Online stores	Fabric stores or online stores

PLEASE NOTE

Aida cloth, used for punch needle work, is not recommended for tufting, as the fabric's weave is too tight for the gun to be able to insert the yarn.

Secondary Backing Fabric

This is the back of your creations! It is applied to the back of the piece during finishing (page 46). Choose it according to its thickness to perfectly camouflage the gluing. Choose a minimum of 7.37 oz. per sq. yd. (250 g per sq. m)

Plain or patterned, the choice is yours! For an aesthetically pleasing finish, I use an off-white 100% cotton fabric that is 8.85 oz. per sq. yd. (300 g per sq. m) (which I buy at a fabric store) to match my herringbone binding tape (page 16). I like my tufted pieces to look as good on the back as they do on the front!

You can also purchase felt from a fabric store (choose a ⅛ in. [2–3 mm] thickness) or non-slip fabric.

Specialty websites sell thick cloth (page 11), but you can also buy it in the upholstery department of a fabric store. Some beautiful fabrics can cost up to $20 a yard.

Yarn

With a tufting gun, you can work with many different yarns. The only requirement is that the yarn must fit perfectly through the needle; typically, this is a medium/worsted to bulky weight yarn. For best results, use finer yarns and work with two or three strands together that equal a medium to bulky weight yarn (page 18). For a rug that is 20 in. (50 cm) a side, plan on using at least 12 oz. (350 g) of yarn.

Traditionally, New Zealand Merino wool is the most widely used in the world of tufting and carpet manufacturing in general. It is sold in cones in specialized stores (page 11). It is generally thick enough to allow you to use just one strand.

However, as wool is expensive and tufted pieces require a lot of it, I suggest you practice with acrylic, a cheap alternative that works perfectly, before investing in quality wools. What's more, acrylic has the advantage of being softer to the touch than wool.

PLEASE NOTE

Certain fibers should not be chosen for tufting: fancy yarns such as faux fur or chenille, crochet thread, macramé cord-type yarns, raffia, and jute.

Here's a table listing the different fibers the gun can tuft. Note that all these yarns hold up perfectly over time if tufted correctly.

Preferred Fibers	Average Price for 1 Ball, 100 g
Acrylic	$3
Alpaca	$10
Cashmere	$15
Mercerized cotton	$2
Merino wool	$6
Mohair	$10
Silk	$9

Rug Binding Tape

Glued around the perimeter of the tufted items, binding tape hides the edges of the primary cloth.

I edge my creations with a 1-in.-wide (2.5-cm-wide) herringbone cotton twill tape—easily purchased from fabric stores. The twill conforms perfectly to the shape of the pieces. I like an off-white color that's close to the backing fabric color. There are many colors to choose from, so have fun matching or mismatching!

To attach the tape, I use a ½ in. (1.5 cm) flat brush (slightly smaller than the width of the tape) and a carpet and flexible flooring adhesive (page 17).

Here's a table showing the length of twill tape required for a round carpet.

Rug Diameter	Length of Tape
19½ in. (50 cm)	63 in. (160 cm)
23½ in. (60 cm)	75 in. (190 cm)
27½ in. (70 cm)	89 in. (225 cm)
31½ in. (80 cm)	100 in. (255 cm)
35½ in. (90 cm)	114 in. (290 cm)
39 in. (100 cm)	126 in. (320 cm)

This binding tape is available by the yard from fabric stores or in rolls on the Internet (page 11).

Glue

To glue on the backing fabric, it is essential to apply a glue designed for laying carpet or flexible flooring. Various brands can be found in any home improvement store.

This type of glue is neither too dense nor too liquid; it is cream-colored and its texture is normally unctuous. It is applied with a trowel or disposable vinyl gloves, and its latex-based composition helps creations retain their suppleness.

For a quality product that will last over time, don't hesitate to pay the price!

PLEASE NOTE

Creating tufted pieces requires a lot of glue. With a small 2 lb. (1 kg) container, you can glue two 20-in-per-side (50-cm-per-side) rugs! Figure on using 12 to 16 oz. (about 400 g) of glue for an item that's about 16 in. (40 cm) per side.

Making Multistrand Balls of Yarn

The gun can insert several strands of yarn into the fabric at once. But this machine is temperamental. If there is the slightest obstacle (for example, if you step on the ball), the gun will pull out the yarn. It is therefore essential that all yarns unwind smoothly. To achieve this, work with double, triple, or quadruple balls that can be made using an easy-to-use ball winder.

When choosing your yarns, start by checking that the combination of strands you plan to use together do not exceed what your gun can handle. For example, for balls made from two yarns, I select a medium weight. Beyond that, the gun will have difficulty inserting the wool correctly into the fabric. If you choose fine- or sport-weight yarns, you can make a ball that combines four different yarns!

1 Attach the winder to the edge of a table.

2 Take the balls of yarn, and pull out the end of the yarn from inside each skein (they will unwind more easily from the inside than from the outside).

3 Place the strands in the guide and then in the notch.

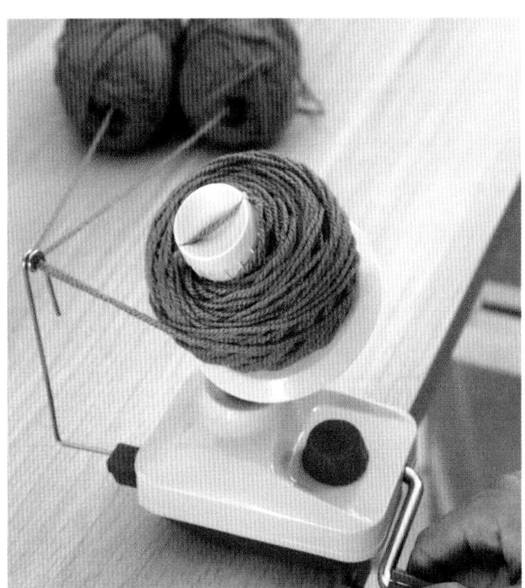

4 Turn the crank slowly, then speed up when you feel the strands are unwinding easily.

5 When the ball is finished, secure the ends of the strands on the inside, and then remove it from the winder.

Building a Frame

The frame is used to hold and stretch the primary tufting cloth. You'll use it each time you tuft. It is very important for the frame to be stable, as you'll be exerting constant pressure on it. It mustn't tip forward!

The drawing of your project must be centered inside the frame. If it's too close to the edge, you risk damaging your gun if it touches the wood. For example, for a piece that is 24 in. (60 cm) on one side, the frame must be at least 30 in. (75 cm) long on that side.

It is quite easy to build a frame. Simply form a square or rectangle with two-by-fours or similar boards and join them together with metal brackets.

TABLETOP FRAME

For small- and medium-sized tufted pieces, I recommend you make a frame that sits on a table. Some online stores sell very good quality kits (you can expect to pay around $70 for a 28-in. (70-cm) frame online.

If you want to make your own, I recommend you choose to make a base that is longer than the other sides, so you can add clamps to hold it firmly to the table.

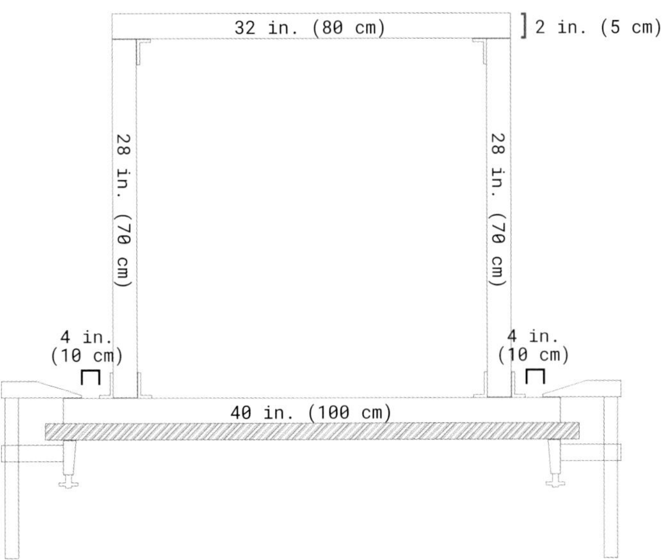

Materials for a 28-in. (70-cm) Frame

For Both Options

- 2 boards (2 × 4 in.), 28 in. (70 cm) long, 2 in. (5 cm) thick (for vertical sides)
- 1 board (2 × 4 in.), 40 in. (100 cm) long, 2 in. (5 cm) thick (for base)
- 1 board (2 × 4 in.), 32 in. (80 cm) long, 2 in. (5 cm) thick (for top)
- 6 metal corner braces
- 2 clamps
- Marker (to mark nail location)
- Hammer
- Screw gun

Option 1 with Nails

- ~ 200 flat head nails, 30 mm × 1.5 mm (to be nailed around the edge of the frame)
- ~ 30 screws, 25 mm × 3.5 mm (to secure the metal braces)

Option 2 with Carpet Gripper

- 10 ft. (3 m) of carpet grippers or carpet tack strips for tufting

Construction

1 Take the 40-in. (100-cm) board and make a mark 4 in. (10 cm) from each end.

2 Place the two 28-in. (70-cm) boards vertically at the marks. Secure them with 4 metal corner braces.

3 Place the 32-in. (80-cm) board on top of the 2 vertical pieces. Secure with the 2 remaining braces.

4 Draw dots in a zigzag line all the way around the frame (about 50 dots per side).

5 With your hammer, tack down the nails at all the dots, letting them protrude about ½ in. (1.5 cm).

6 Finish by securing the frame to the table using the 2 clamps.

Option 2

If you don't have the patience to add all the nails to your own frame, there are ready-to-use carpet grippers available on the Internet. Each retailer offers different sizes. Be sure that you get enough to go around the entire frame. For a better fit, the strips can easily be cut to size with a small saw.

Start by working steps 1 to 3, then attach the carpet grippers all around the frame. Make sure that the nails face outward. As before, secure the frame to the table using the 2 clamps.

FLOOR FRAME

If you want to produce medium-sized pieces from 3 to 6 ft. (1 to 2 m) long, you can make a large frame that stands on the floor. It will lean slightly against a wall.

For an even more stable structure or for tufting larger pieces, you will need to design legs. In this case, you won't be able to move it, so plan on finding a dedicated space for it.

To learn more about the process of building a floor frame (quite similar to that of the tabletop frame), I recommend No Fun Studio's YouTube tutorial titled "How to Build a Rug Making Frame—Step by Step Guide for Height Adjustable Tufting Setup." In this video, you'll also find explanations for building stable legs.

Stretching the Cloth

This step can absolutely not be skipped, and it requires a lot of patience! The cloth must be perfectly stretched before tufting. To make the task easier, some tufting cloth has woven marking lines (page 12) to ensure correct placement.

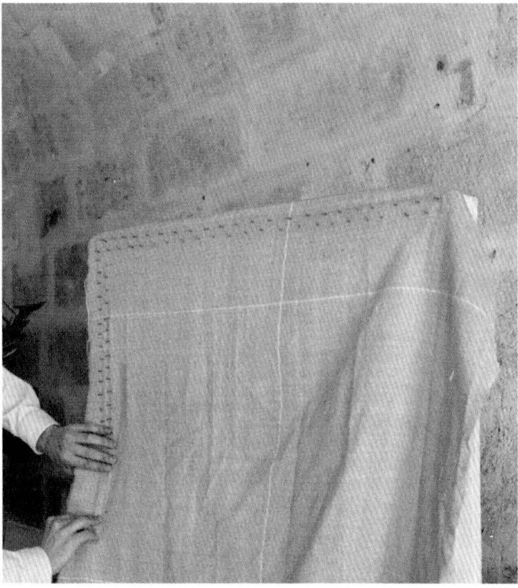

1 Start by placing the cloth on the top of the frame. Gradually place it over the nails, making sure it's taut.

2 Once the first side has been attached, continue with a vertical side. Be sure the marking lines are straight. If they are curved, the cloth is crooked, and you may not be able to tuft straight lines. You must undo part of the cloth to readjust its position.

3 Continue by pulling the second vertical side over the tacks.

4 Pull taut on the last side. To ensure that the cloth is stretched tight enough, run your hand over all sides. The entire surface should be perfectly taut, like the skin of a drum. If you feel that some places are a bit loose, remove a small part of the cloth from the tacks and pull it tighter until the entire surface is quite taut.

I Have a Problem with My Cloth!

My cloth is tearing. If you're using special tufting cloth and it's tearing, it may be due to the way you tuft. Either you're not going fast enough for the gun and you're inserting too much yarn in the same place, or you're making curves too quickly and the scissors are cutting the stitches (for cut pile guns).

My cloth is becoming slack. Preparing the cloth is the most important step, as it's very awkward and difficult to tuft on a badly stretched cloth. This problem must be solved beforehand, as continuing to tighten the fabric during the process could distort the design. A well-stretched cloth, like the skin of a drum, should not relax.

My cloth has a hole in it. When there is strain put on the same area over too long a period, the cloth may become slack and get a hole in it. If the hole is smaller than ¼ to ⅜ in. (1 cm), you can try repairing the weave with some thread to reshape it. See the AJ MAKES YouTube tutorial titled "How to Patch a Hole in Your Tufting Fabric."

However, now you cannot use the tufting gun on this area. Use a large needle to manually pull the yarn through the fabric to form a loop! Cut the loops after gluing the back of the piece to prevent the yarn from escaping.

If you have opted to use burlap, which is stiffer than tufting cloth, there is a greater risk of creating holes. It is therefore advisable not to make large patterns, and to pass the gun through the fabric as few times as possible.

Learning to Use Your Tufting Gun

Is your cloth stretched taut and your balls of yarn all wound? Now you are ready to try out your tufting gun!

UNDERSTANDING HOW YOUR TUFTING GUN WORKS

The tufting gun is a complex machine with many small mechanisms and electronic components.

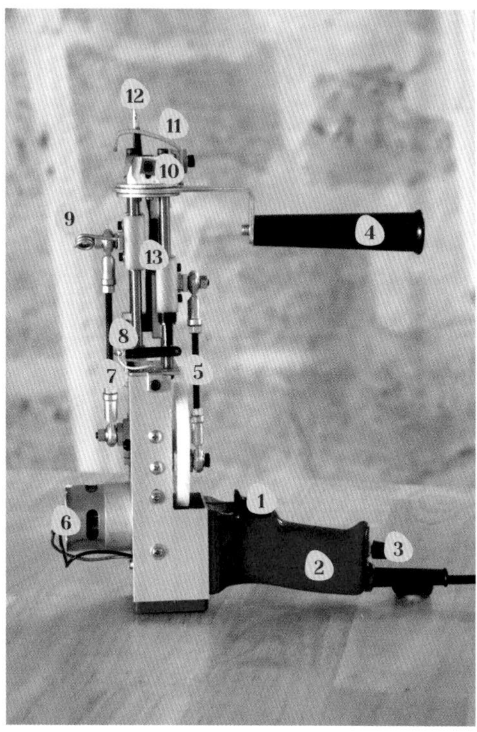

1. Trigger (to activate the gun)
2. Handle (to hold the gun)
3. Speed regulator (to adjust the speed)
4. Swivel handle (to support the gun)
5. Lower arm
6. Motor
7. Upper arm
8. Scissor opener
9. Yarn guide (first place where yarn is to be inserted)
10. Scissor closer
11. Foot or buffer
12. Needle (second place where yarn is to be inserted)
13. Scissors

Tufting Safely without Disturbing Others!

Never point the gun at yourself or anyone else. The needle and scissors can cause injury.

If you have long hair, tie it up. It could get caught in the gears of the gun.

It is better if you don't wear scarves, earrings, or necklaces, as they could also get caught in the gears.

When handling the gun, always make sure it is switched off (red indicator light is off at the rear). Only switch on the gun when you're ready to tuft.

When you're not using your gun, place it upright or lay it on a soft surface (such as foam) to avoid damaging the delicate mechanisms.

It is strongly recommended that you wear a mask and protective goggles, as the gun continuously sprays yarn particles.

A tufting gun is noisy. If you have sensitive hearing, wear noise-cancelling headphones, available from home improvement stores.

Vibrations from the frame can be disturbing for people sharing your space or for your neighbors in an apartment building. Be reasonable and don't tuft at night! To reduce vibrations from a floor frame, place vibration isolation pads and non-slip pads, used for washing machines, under the frame.

To understand how your gun works (only when the gun is switched off!), turn the large white gear and watch what happens: one part moves forward, and the needle moves back. For the cut loop model, the scissors advance, close, and retract. The loop pile gun simply has a plunger to insert the wool into the fabric, without cutting it. You'll notice that the upper and lower arms of the gun move back and forth.

< SCISSORS ON THE TUFTING GUN

TIP

To properly adjust the needle height of your gun (and therefore of the pile), I recommend the Tuftinglove YouTube channel, where you can find their step-by-step guide to adjusting the gun.

INSERTING THE YARN

To insert the yarn into the gun, a little tool known as a needle threader (available from fabric stores or specialized online stores) is handy. Alternatively, a simple paper clip will do just fine. Simply unfold the first part and form a small hook!

The yarn must pass through two holes, first the guide and then the needle.

1 Take the ends from inside the ball (so it unwinds more easily). Position the needle threader or paper clip through the needle (from bottom to top) and through the guide, then insert the yarn in the threader or paperclip.

2 Pull up to bring the yarn strands through the holes.

GOOD POSTURE IS ESSENTIAL

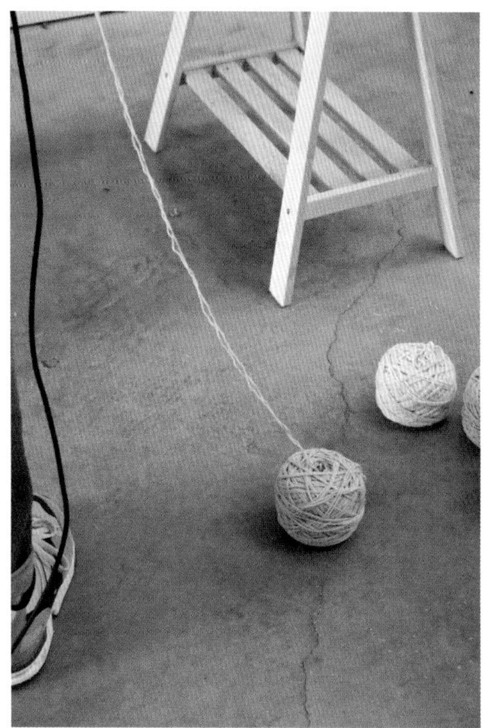

Stand as upright as possible to avoid back pain, and place the gun level with your chest, always perpendicular to the cloth, to minimize strain on your arms.

If you're right-handed, hold the gun in your right hand, with the swivel handle in your left; if left-handed, hold the gun in your left hand, with the swivel handle in your right. The hand holding the gun will steer it.

Place the ball of yarn at your feet, on your right side if right-handed and left side if left-handed. Make sure there are no obstacles that would keep the yarn from unwinding.

TIP

A standard gun weighs around 3.3 lbs. (1.5 kg). Its weight and its vibrations can cause wrist pain. To spare my wrists, I take breaks every 30 minutes, which also gives my arms a breather and the machine a rest. I then take the opportunity to check that the gun is well lubricated.

DRAWING YOUR FIRST LINES

Before tackling curves, you'll need to master straight lines. Practice makes perfect!

1 Using a marker, draw straight vertical lines on the cloth.

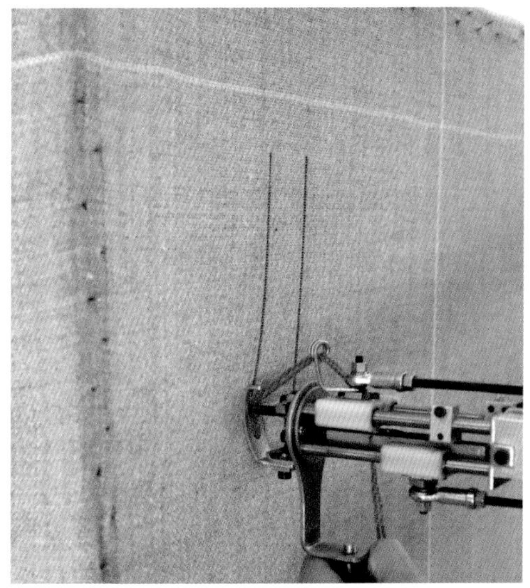

2 Tuft from bottom to top. With the gun switched off, set the dial to the lowest speed, push the needle into the fabric, apply light pressure on the fabric, and switch on the gun.

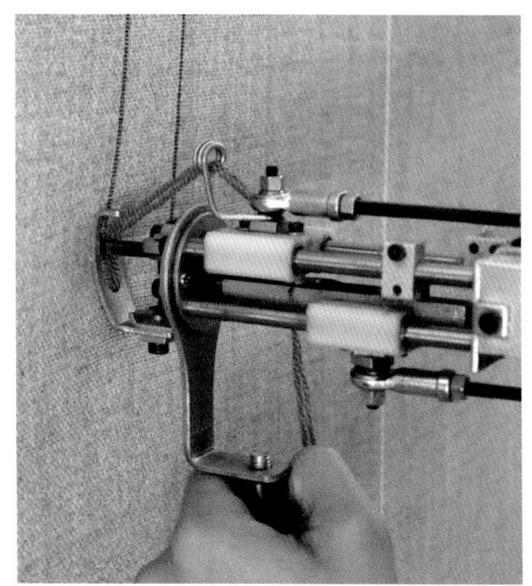

3 Keeping your finger pressed on the trigger, tuft the first line. Pay attention to pressure and speed. Once the first line has been tufted, remove the gun. See how it looks on the front of the fabric.

REMINDER

Loop pile guns require you to manually cut the tufted line with scissors. Cut pile models do it for you.

4 Insert the gun about ⅛ in. (3 mm) from the base of the line you've just tufted and make a second line. Continue making lines side by side until you've formed a square or rectangle.

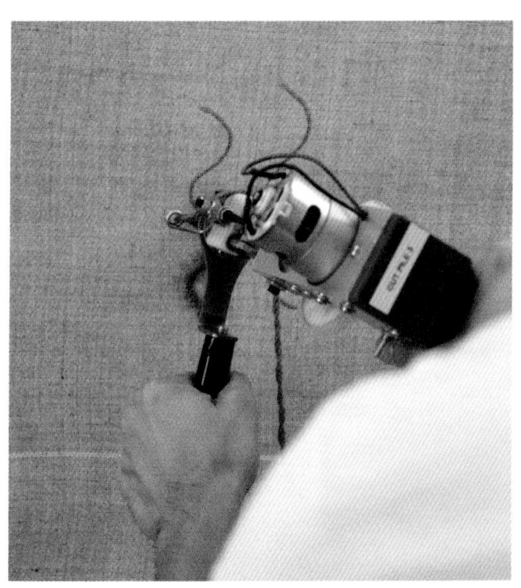

5 Once you're comfortable with straight lines, move on to vertical, wavy curved lines. The hand holding the gun, not the swivel handle, steers to follow the curve! Don't get discouraged. Perfect curves are difficult to achieve, especially the curves of a circle.

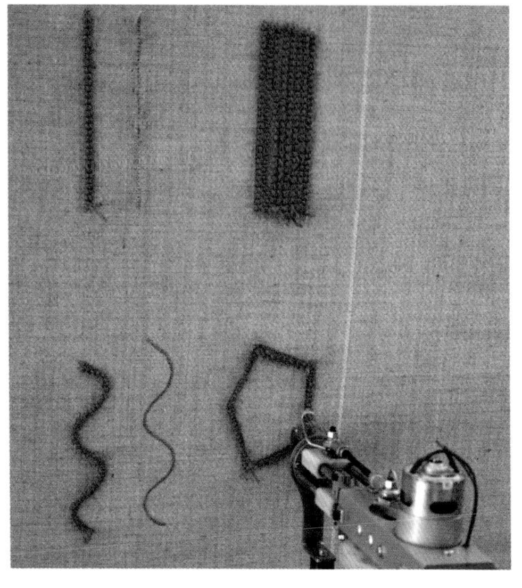

6 Finish these practice steps by tufting a polygon. Start by working on drawing its outline. To closely follow the shape, think about tufting in a staccato fashion (pressing, then quickly releasing the trigger) to adjust the tilt of the handle more often.

If the lines are well filled in, congratulations, you've succeeded! If they're sparse, you're either not applying enough pressure, or you're going too fast. Practice to find your ideal rhythm. On the back, a well-tufted line looks like a braid.

^

ON THE BACK SIDE: ON THE LEFT, A PERFECT LINE; ON THE RIGHT, A SPARSE LINE DUE TO INSUFFICIENT PRESSURE

^

ON THE FRONT SIDE: ON THE LEFT, HOW AN IMPERFECT LINE LOOKS; ON THE RIGHT, HOW A GOOD LINE LOOKS

FINDING YOUR CRUISING SPEED

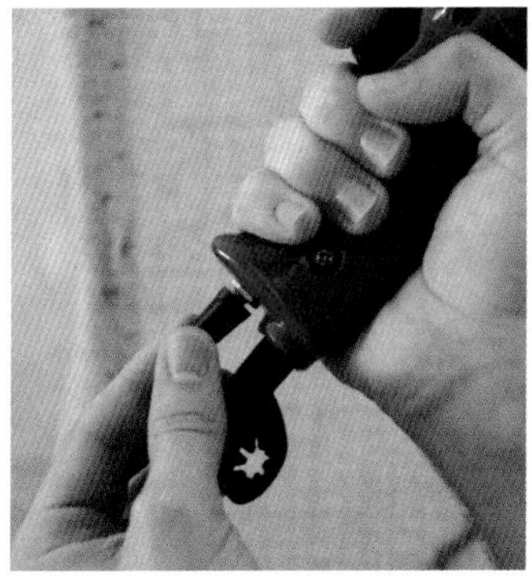

< KNOB TO ADJUST GUN SPEED

When you first start practicing, you'll feel that the gun wants to move forward on its own. You will need to find the right speed for the yarn to insert properly. If you don't exert enough pressure on the fabric, the gun will not insert the yarn properly, and if you don't go fast enough, too much yarn may be inserted in the same place and weaken the fabric.

Once you've become proficient with your gun, you can gradually increase its speed as you work, by turning the knob. Personally, I never use maximum speed, as the gun is uncontrollable!

When I'm starting a project or outlining a shape, I always use the minimum speed. I increase it a little for repetitive tasks, for example, when I'm filling a large flat area with color.

ESTABLISHING THE IDEAL LINE SPACING

Finding the perfect spacing between two lines is very important. Lines should not be too close together to avoid dense areas, and not too far apart to avoid hollow spaces. To ensure this, constantly check the front of the cloth by running your hand over it.

If the result is not optimal, don't be discouraged. This stage requires a great deal of patience. Regular practice will help you become skilled at using the machine.

>
ON THE BACK:
PERFECTLY
SPACED LINES

<
ON THE FRONT:
A DENSE,
SHAGGY LOOK

F.Y.I.

Line spacing varies depending on the type of yarn and needle length.

DAILY CARE OF YOUR TUFTING GUN

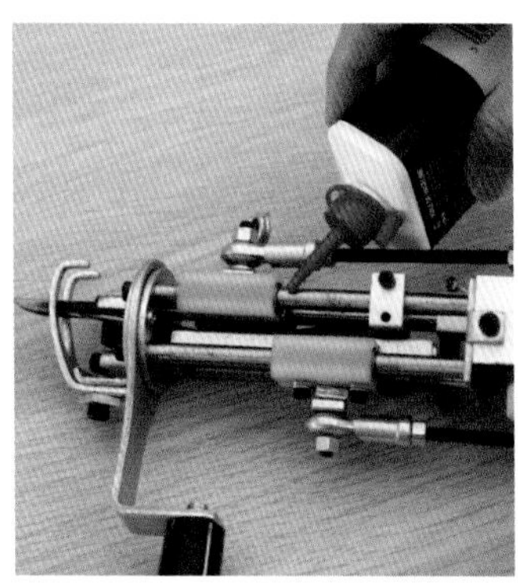

After each use, don't forget to clean your gun and remove wool fluff with some kind of brush or a small air gun.

Regularly check if your gun needs lubricating. To do this, with the gun switched off, touch the moving parts (the bars on the gun and ball shapes at the ends of the arms). If they are dry, add a few drops of lubricant. Remember also to lubricate the parts that are hidden when stopped, by turning the white gear to make them visible.

As I use my gun daily, I go through these steps every day. When I'm doing a lot of tufting, I sometimes even check while I'm working, to see that the gun is well lubricated, and that lint isn't getting in the way of the mechanism. The better you take care of your gun, the longer it will last!

Help, There's a Problem with My Tufting Gun!

The scissors on my cut pile gun don't cut. This is the most common problem encountered with this type of gun. First, check the movement of the scissors. With the gun off, turn the white gear 360° and see if the scissors open and close. If they don't, follow the YouTube tutorial "Scissors Are Not Closing, Scissors Not Cutting" on the Tuftinglove channel, which explains very well what to do.

My gun runs by itself. If your gun continues to run even though the trigger is not engaged, there's a little too much pressure in the handle. With the gun off, unscrew the handle screw (top corner) just a bit. The gun should stop working on its own.

My gun is beeping. With the gun off, make sure nothing is hampering the movement of the gears (yarn, hair, etc.). If anything is in the way, gently remove it with your fingers. Otherwise, the gun may not be sufficiently lubricated. With the gun off, add lubricant on the parts subject to stress (bars and gears).

Copying a Design

First, I always plan out the designs I want to create by drawing my ideas in a sketchbook while thinking about a color scheme. Once the design has been chosen, it must be copied onto the cloth stretched over the frame.

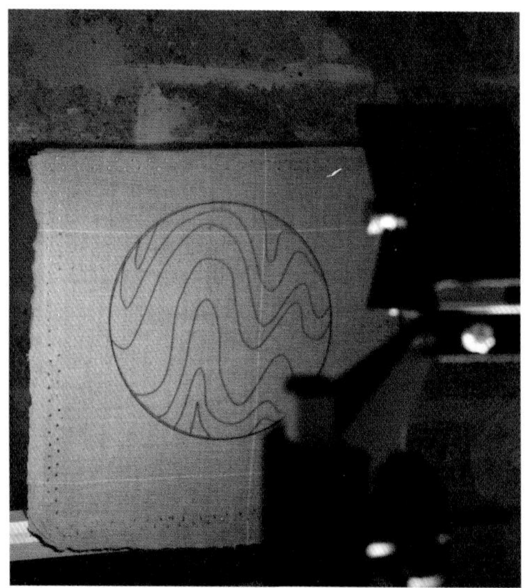

If you choose the overhead or video projector option, be sure to print the design on transparent sheets beforehand. It is very important that you trace or project a flipped image of the design so that it's facing the right way (in the projects, the templates are shown flipped). Make sure you keep a reminder next to your frame, because, believe me, this is a fairly common mistake!

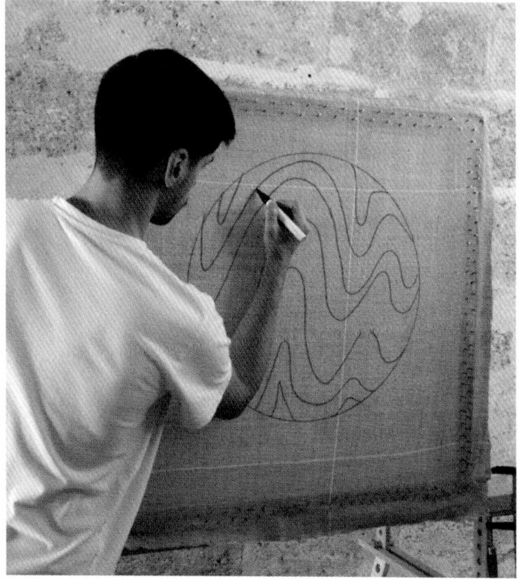

1 With a large Sharpie-type marker, copy the drawing onto the cloth by freehand or by using an overhead projector (like those used in classrooms) or a video projector connected to a computer. When drawing the outlines of the design, always leave an open space (about 6 in. [15 cm]) on the fabric to test the gun.

2 Write down the names of the colors on the transferred design, so you won't make a mistake when you tuft!

WHAT WILL IT COST?

On the Internet, you'll find used overhead projectors for around $50. Newer machines cost considerably more (around $320). Small, computer-connected projectors are available at affordable prices (starting at around $40).

Tufting Your First Piece

Once the yarn is ready and the design has been copied onto the cloth, it's time to tuft!

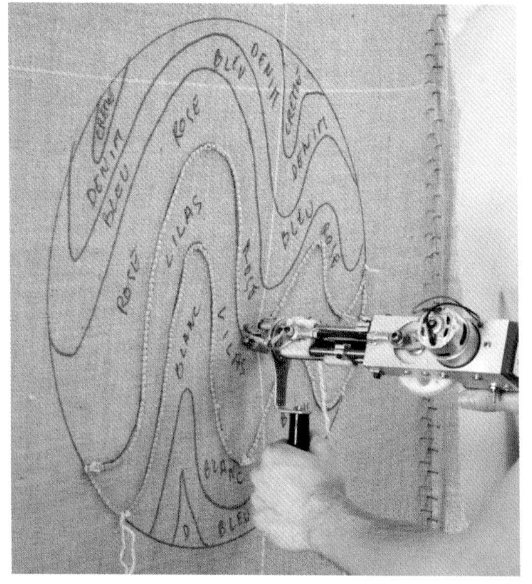

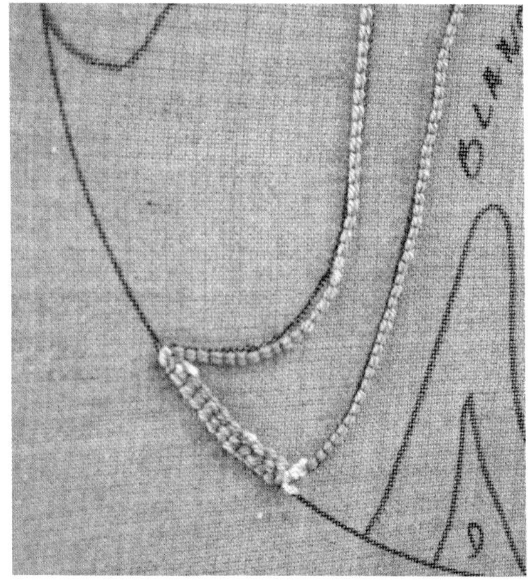

1 First, test the gun on some empty space left on the cloth. Check that everything works and that the yarns insert perfectly. Take this opportunity to tuft a few lines with all the yarn colors to make sure the color palette you've chosen works well.

2 Start by working around the outline of one shape to define the area to be tufted.

3 On the edges of the design, where the fabric will be folded for finishing (page 46), I strongly recommend tufting a few extra lines. The yarn should be very dense on the edges so that the primary cloth is not too visible. Don't neglect this step!

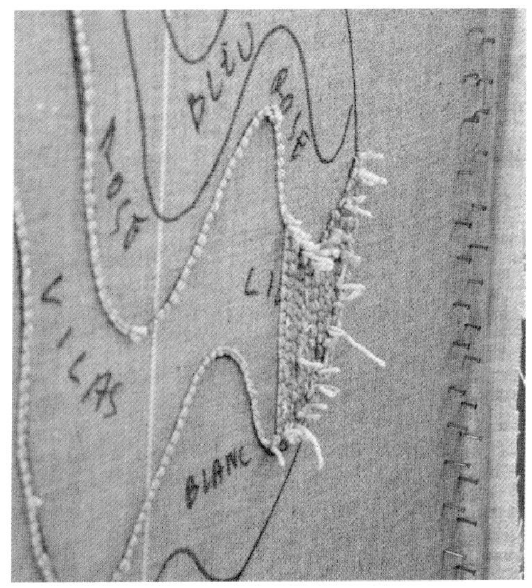

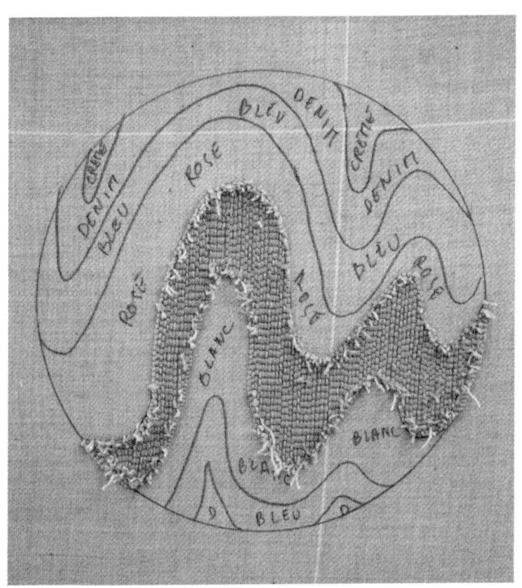

4 Tuft the outlined area from bottom to top to fill it completely. Make lines side by side, leaving a very slight space between them. From time to time, check the tufting density by touching the front of the piece. Continue until the first shape is filled.

TIP

If you feel any hollows on the front, close up the space between lines by tufting a new line to fill it. If, however, the yarn is packed in too tightly, space out the lines slightly. If the yarn is too concentrated in one spot, remove a few strands with tweezers.

5 Once the first shape is complete, stand facing the front of the piece and pick up a pair of scissors (regular or duckbill). To ensure that the yarn strands don't mix with the other colors, you'll need to trim the shape—take your time or you'll put a hole in the primary tufting cloth. This step is optional, but highly recommended if you want an impeccable finish, and will save you time during the final steps!

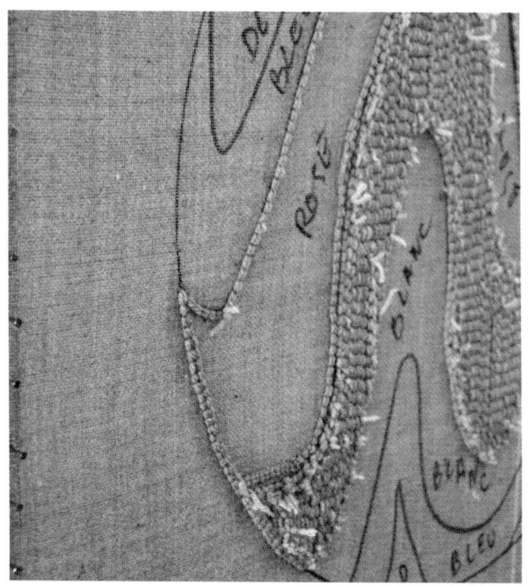

6 Change yarn and tuft the outline of the second shape.

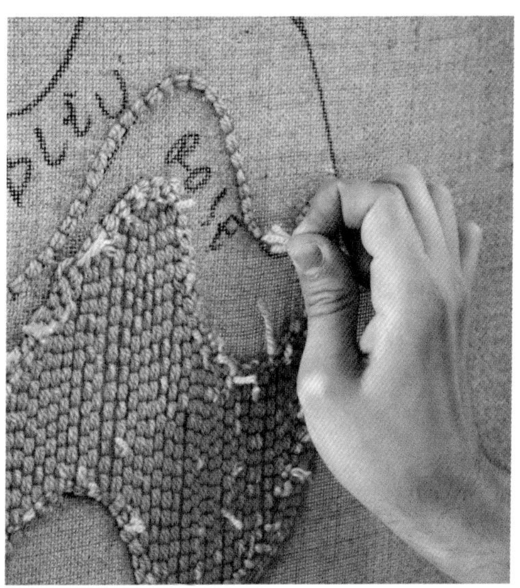

7 If you have not tufted a part of the design correctly, simply remove the yarn strands by hand or with tweezers.

8 Once the piece is fully tufted, remove any yarn that sticks out by cutting it off with the scissors you prefer. The surface must be as flat as possible to proceed to the gluing stage, so be sure there are no protruding strands.

Finishing Steps

Don't be careless about the finishing steps. They are what will make your piece look its best and have a long life.

THE BACK SIDE

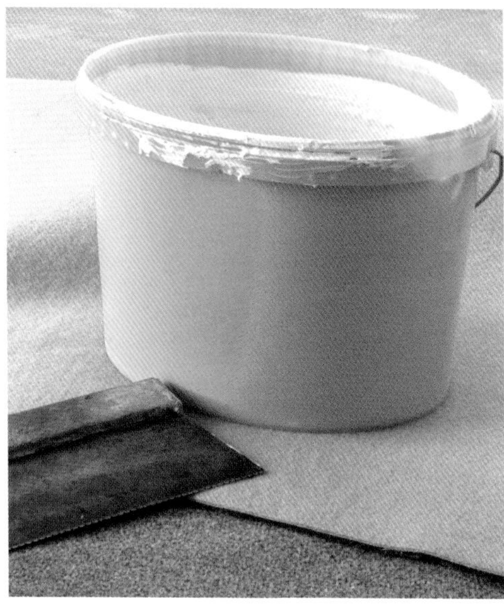

Once the tufting stage is complete, you will move on to the first step in finishing: gluing the back of the piece.

Backing Fabric

Materials

- Thick cotton fabric (allow 2 in. [5 cm] extra fabric on each side of the design)
- Glue for carpet and flexible flooring (allow 14 oz. [400 g] of glue for a 16 in. [40 cm] square piece)
- Trowel to adhere the fabric to the glue
- Disposable vinyl gloves or putty knife (or palette knife) to apply glue
- Regular scissors

IMPORTANT

You'll be gluing your piece while it is on the frame, so don't take the cloth off during this step, or your piece won't retain its original shape! You can, however, lay the frame down by removing the clamps so you can apply the glue horizontally.

1 Apply glue to the back of the piece using a small putty knife or disposable gloves to protect your hands.

2 To ensure that the edges fold over easily, do not apply glue to a ½-in. (1.5-cm) border around the rug. If you use this method, the binding tape will glue on smoothly.

3 Place the secondary backing fabric onto the glue. Secure with masking tape.

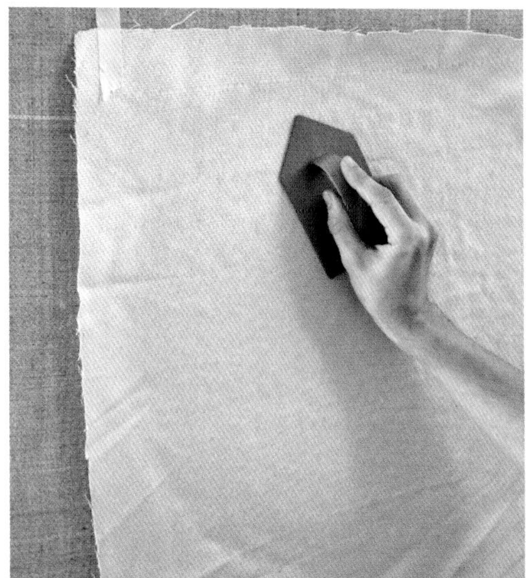

4 Press a trowel, float, or the flat of your hand over the fabric to ensure perfect adhesion.

5 Let the fabric dry overnight in a well-ventilated room, without removing it from the frame. Run your hand over the fabric to make sure the glue is completely dry. If it's cold or a little damp, it is not yet ready. When the glue is completely dry, remove the cloth from the frame. Your tufted piece begins to take shape! All that remains is to finish off the back.

Materials

- Rug binding tape
- Glue for carpet and flexible flooring (page 17)
- Flat brush, ½ in. (1.5 cm) wide
- Regular scissors
- Lighter (optional)

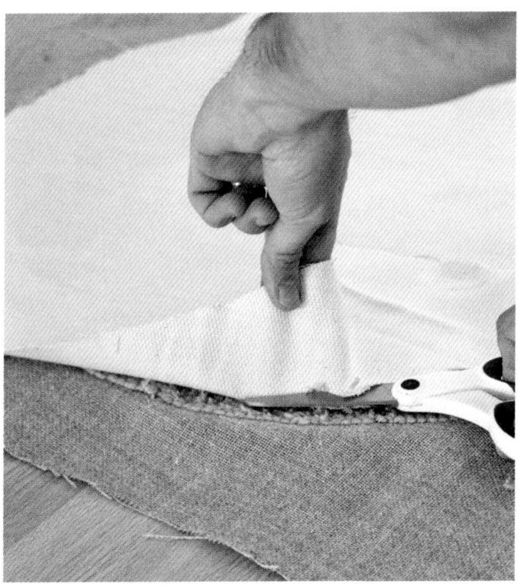

1 Turn the piece over and trim off the excess thick fabric on the back. The unglued area from step 2 on page 47 should be visible.

2 Cut the tufting cloth, leaving a ½ to ¾ in. (1.5 to 2 cm) border all around. It will be folded over and hidden under the binding tape.

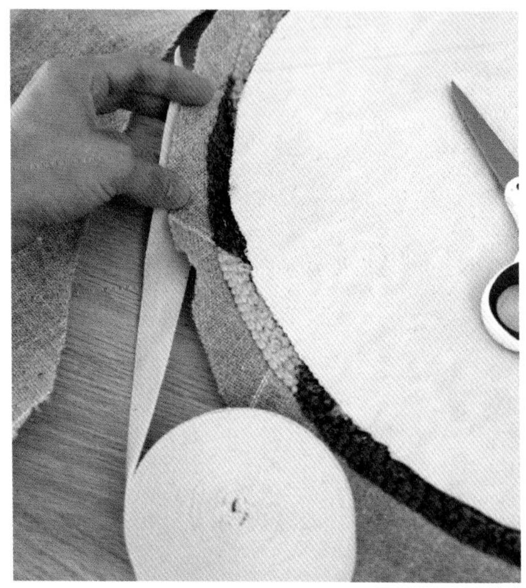

3 Cut the required length of binding tape, using four pieces for a square or rectangular piece, and one for a round piece. Cut it a bit longer for a little leeway (approx. 4 in. [10 cm]). For a 20-in. (50-cm) piece, you'll need 63 in. (160 cm).

4 Special tufting fabric has only one drawback: the threads unravel very easily if you pull on them. Run the flame of a lighter very quickly along the edge so that the fibers curl up and harden.

5 With your scissors, make notches in the corners to fold over the fabric more easily. For a rounded carpet, make notches every 2 in. (5 cm).

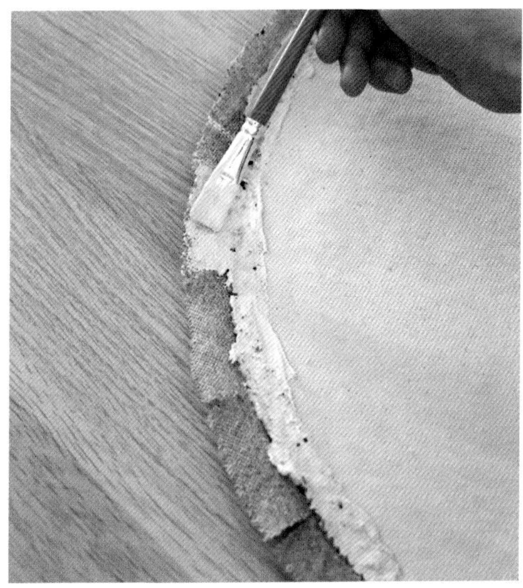

6 Using the flat brush, apply glue to the tufted area not covered by the backing fabric.

7 Still using the flat brush, apply a thin layer of glue without clumps to the edge of the tufting cloth.

8 Fold the tufting cloth over, gluing it to the back with the help of the brush. Continue until the entire edge is glued down.

9 Glue on the binding tape section by section. Using a flat brush, apply glue to the tape for about 8 in. (20 cm).

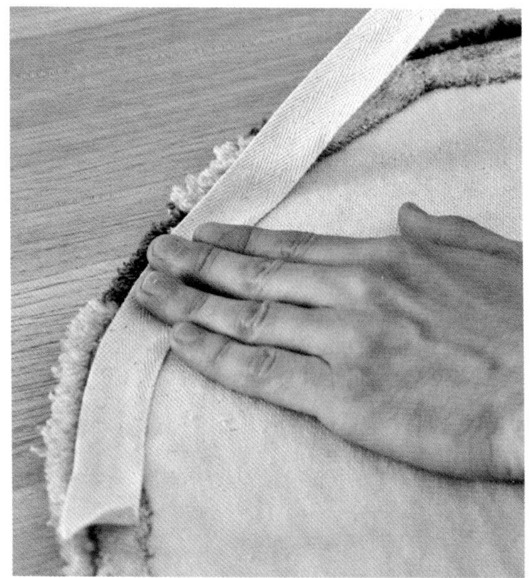

10 Glue the tape to the edge of the piece, covering the primary tufting cloth. Continue until you've gone all around the edge of the piece.

TIP

To hold the binding tape in place and prevent it from moving while you're gluing, I recommend using weights, such as books. This will help you flawlessly apply the tape.

11 Join the two ends by pinching the base of the seam. Use a clip if needed. Let dry for one day.

12 When the glue is completely dry (see above), turn over your piece and tackle the final step: finishing the front!

THE FRONT SIDE

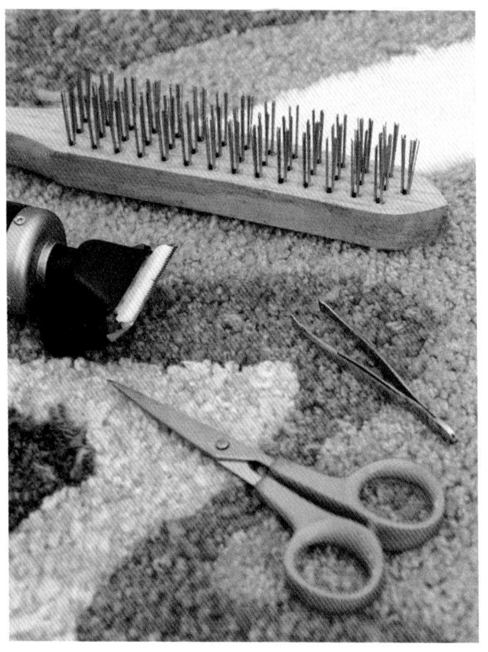

The finishing steps on the front side smooth out and reveal the beautiful shapes of the tufted piece.

Please note that these last steps are only possible if you've used a cut pile gun and not a loop pile gun. Brushing a looped rug would be pointless and could damage it!

Brushing

This step is optional, but it does help to obtain an even, tufted texture, like the fur on a stuffed animal.

I recommend a wire-bristle brush (they cost $4 to $10 in home improvement stores). Metal bristles pull apart the fibers and make them softer.

For impeccable results, brush vigorously from the center toward the outside edge. This step requires some energy!

PLEASE NOTE

Do not brush toward yourself, as this may cause injury. The metal bristles are sharp, so watch your fingers!

Shearing and Trimming

Once you've finished brushing, it's time to move on to the final steps: shearing and trimming. Be careful, a hole can happen very quickly!

Depending on the size of your project, you have several choices when it comes to shearing.

- For small- and medium-sized pieces (less than a yard/meter long), I recommend small clippers designed for pet grooming (available online, on specialized tufting sites, and at pet stores). Don't try to make do with hair clippers—they are not powerful enough.

^ SHEEP SHEARS

- For larger pieces, invest in carpet carving clippers or professional sheep shears. A little heavy and very noisy, sheep shears are ideal for shearing dense yarn. When handling this machine, be meticulous and don't go too fast so as not to puncture the fabric.

  The shears come at all prices, but I'd advise you not to limit yourself to the low-cost models, as you risk unpleasant surprises (such as a very short lifespan). Be sure to read the online reviews. I invested in a mid-range machine at around $80, bought on Amazon.

● If you don't want to buy carpet carving clippers right away, this step can be performed with duckbill scissors. This will take much longer, of course, and the result will be less smooth.

Like the tufting gun, the clippers need to be cleaned and lubricated each time they are used.

1 Shear very carefully, a little at a time. Start by trimming around the edges of the piece, avoiding clipping too fast and in long lines, so as not to cut little grooves or make a hole. Place the clipper guide flat against the surface of the piece and maintain constant pressure and speed.

2 Finish by trimming to repair small imperfections. Using the corner of the carpet carving clippers, cleanly trim the edges of the shapes again. As before, go slowly!

3 If any colors get mixed together, use tweezers to move the strands to the correct place.

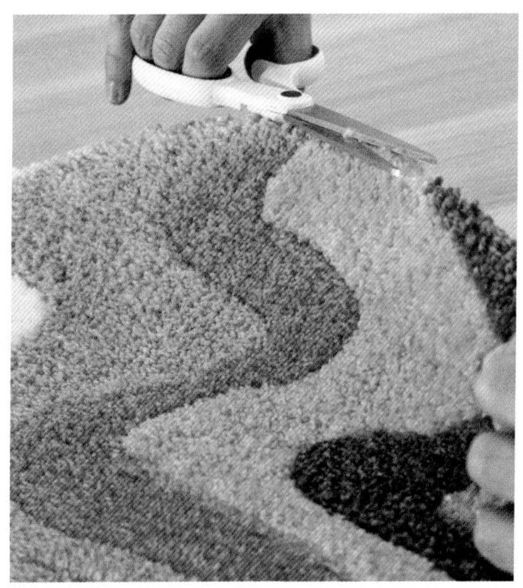

4 Use the scissors to even out any protruding strands along the edges.

Taking Care of Your Tufted Pieces

Once you've finished your tufted piece, it must be vacuumed to remove any loose fibers. The best way to do this is to use the brush function on your vacuum cleaner, but you can also opt for a manual carpet shaver.

Your tufted pieces cannot be machine-washed. In the event of a stain, clean quickly with a damp cloth and leave to air dry.

For the first few weeks, your carpet will lose fibers whenever it is rubbed. This is perfectly normal! All you need to do is vacuum it regularly. Over time, it will become softer and more beautiful!

Hanging Your Work of Art

Here's a simple way to hang tufted wall decor without a dowel.

Materials

- 63/100 in. (16 mm) brass-plated triangle picture frame hanger with two holes
- Sewing thread in the same color as the binding tape
- Sewing needle (must fit through the holes in the hanger)
- Felt-tip pen
- Regular scissors

1 Turn the piece over and choose where to attach the hanger.

TIP

To make the fastener invisible on the front, place its bottom at the inside edge of the binding tape.

2 Using the felt-tip pen, mark a dot in each hole. Remove the hanger.

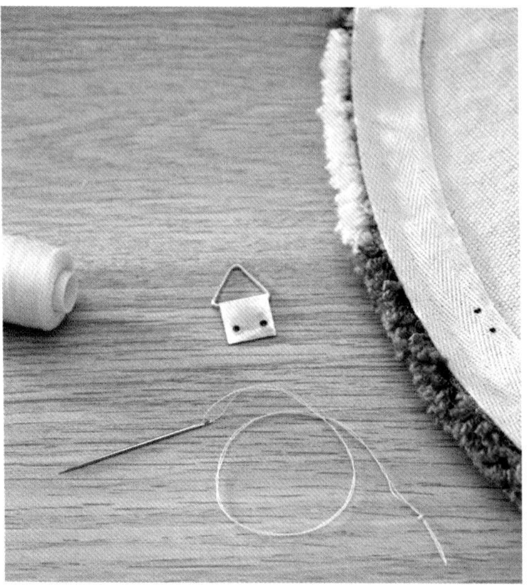

3 Cut 16 in. (40 cm) of sewing thread and insert it through the eye of the needle. Fold in half and double knot the ends.

4 Insert the needle through the front of the rug to go through the marker dot on the back. Pull the thread through to the double knot.

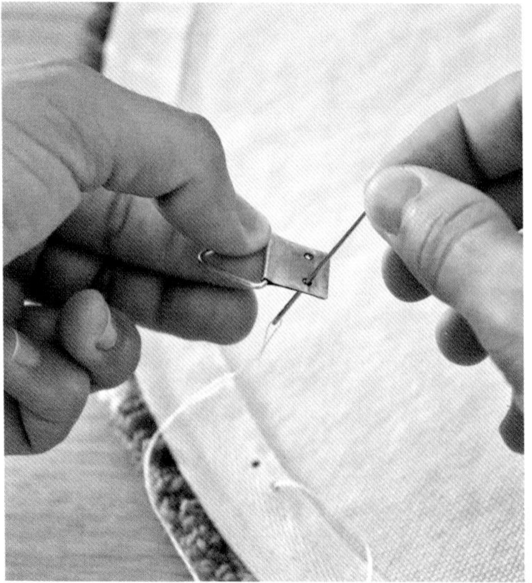

5 Pass the needle through the first hole in the hanger.

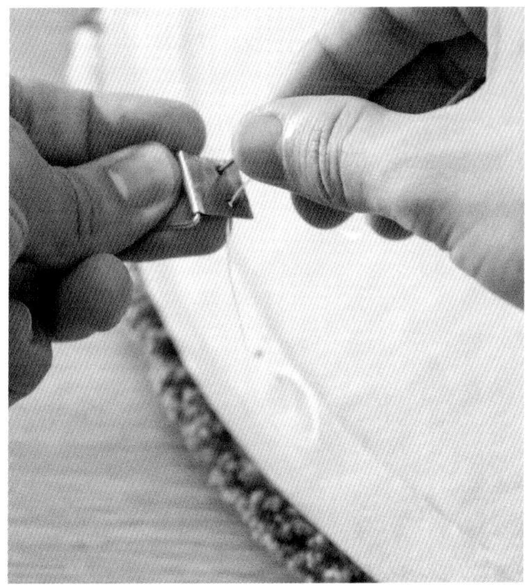

6 Bring the needle down and out through the second hole.

7 Insert the needle into the second marker dot and pull the thread through.

8 Repeat steps 4 to 7 until the fastener is secure. I usually do this five times.

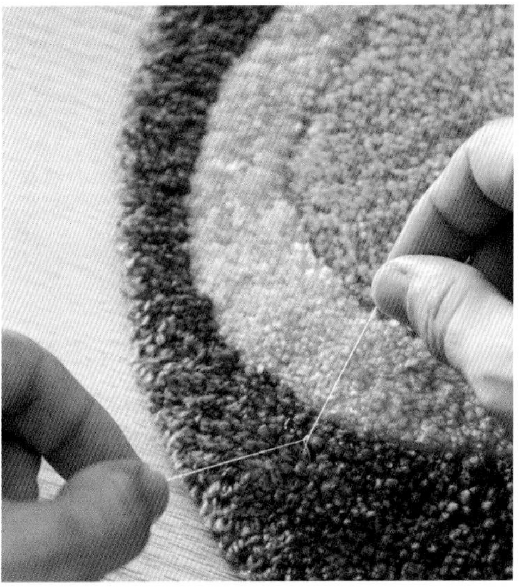

9 Tie a double knot at the front of the rug to secure it. Trim any ends that may stick out.

Projects

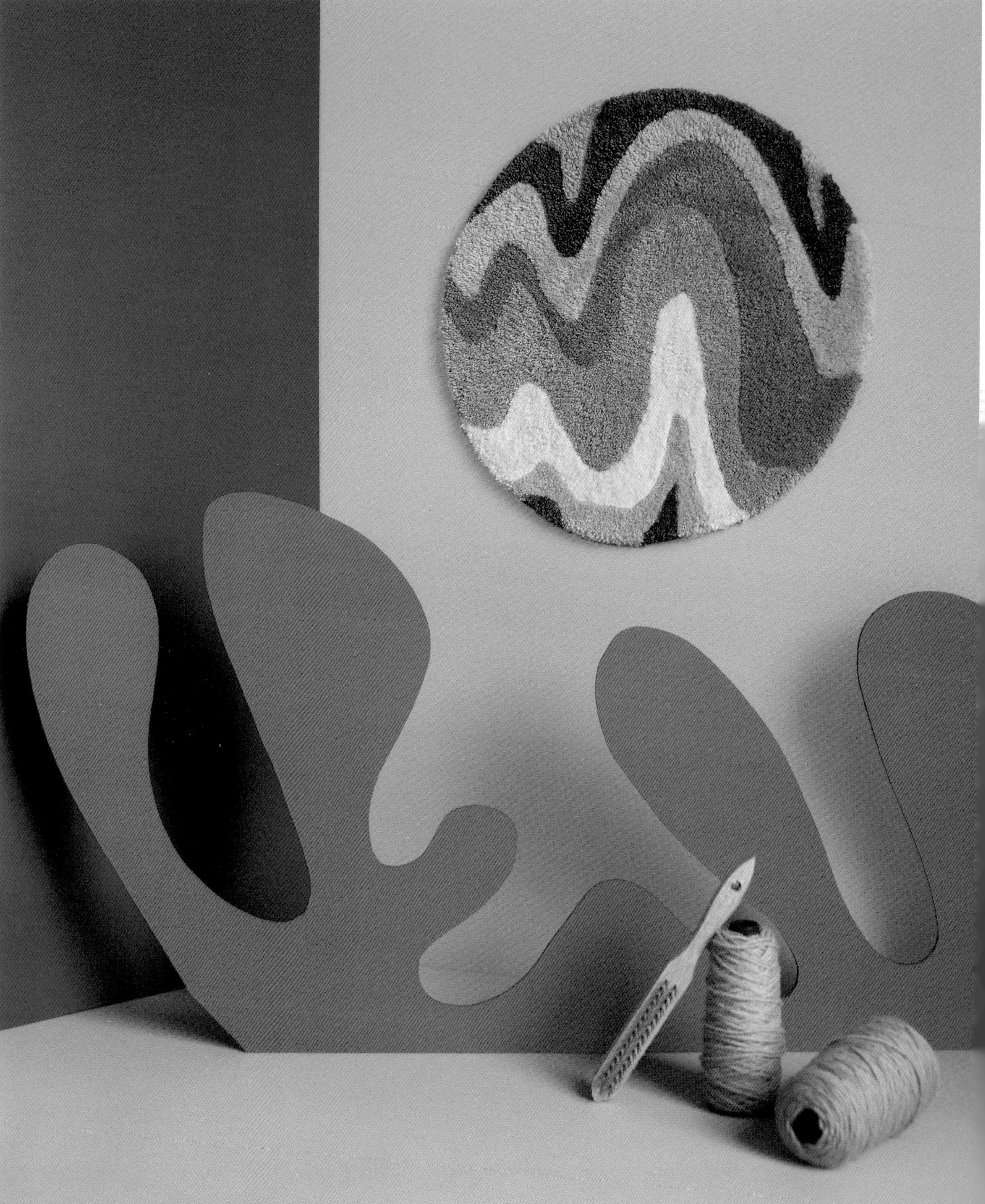

Difficulty ** Diameter: 20 in. (50 cm)

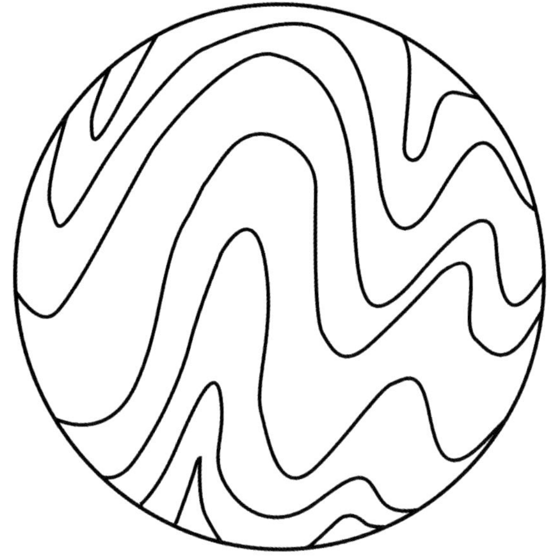

Materials

- Basic materials (pages 8 to 17)
- Large compass

Yarn

Color	Yarn Brand	Weight of Yarn Ball	Qty.	No. of 3.5 oz (100 g) Double Yarn Balls Needed	Actual Qty. Used
#41 LIGHT BLUE	Katia Merino Baby	1.8 oz. (50 g)	2	1	1.7 oz. (49 g)
#44 MEDIUM BLUE	Katia Merino Baby	1.8 oz. (50 g)	2	1	1 oz. (27 g)
#3 BISQUE	Pingouin Pingo First	1.8 oz. (50 g)	2	1	0.2 oz. (5 g)
#3 CREAM	Katia 100% Merino No. 3	1.8 oz. (50 g)	2	1	1.1 oz. (30 g)
#66 LIGHT MAUVE	Katia Merino Baby	1.8 oz. (50 g)	2	1	1.7 oz. (48 g)
#77 SALMON	Katia Merino Baby	1.8 oz. (50 g)	2	1	1.7 oz. (48 g)

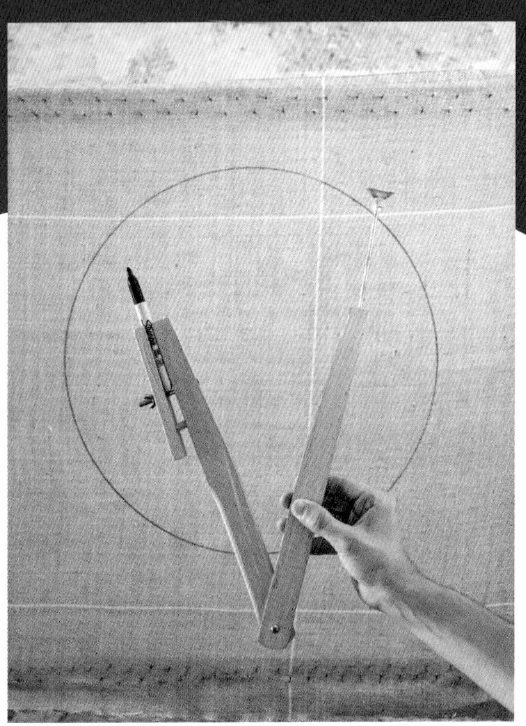

1 Using a large compass, draw a circle 20 in. (50 cm) in diameter on the primary cloth stretched on the frame.

2 Using a marker, copy the design and indicate the colors.

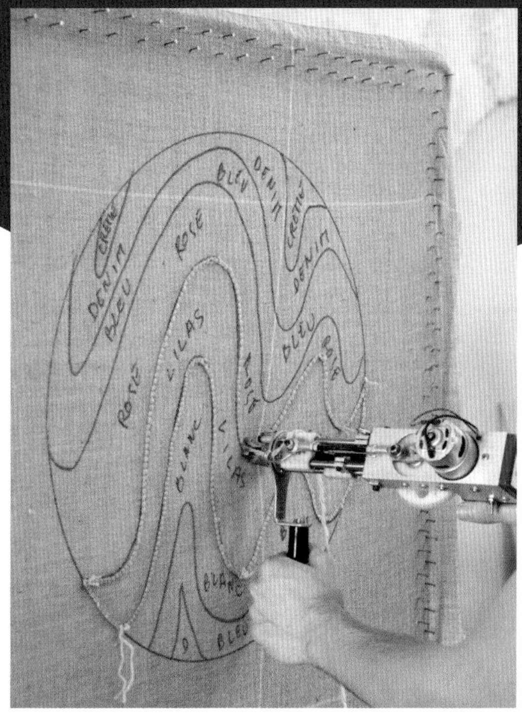

3 Make the double yarn balls needed per the table on page 65.

4 Start by tufting the outline of the light-mauve shape. In the curve, briefly squeeze then release the trigger to work in short spurts.

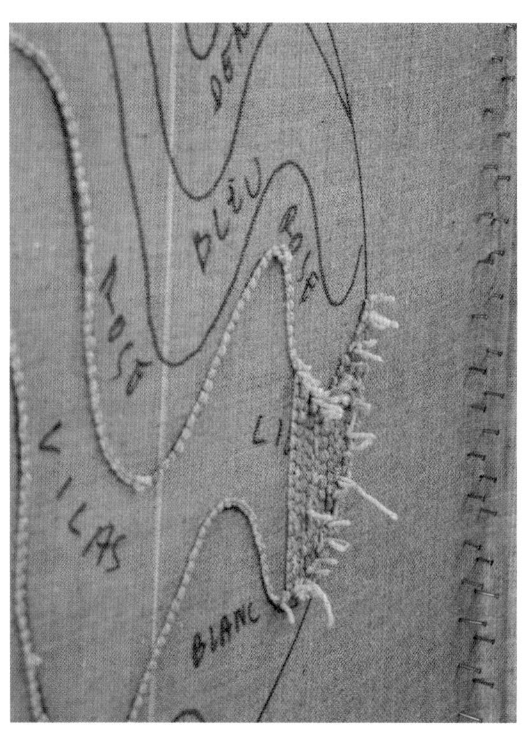

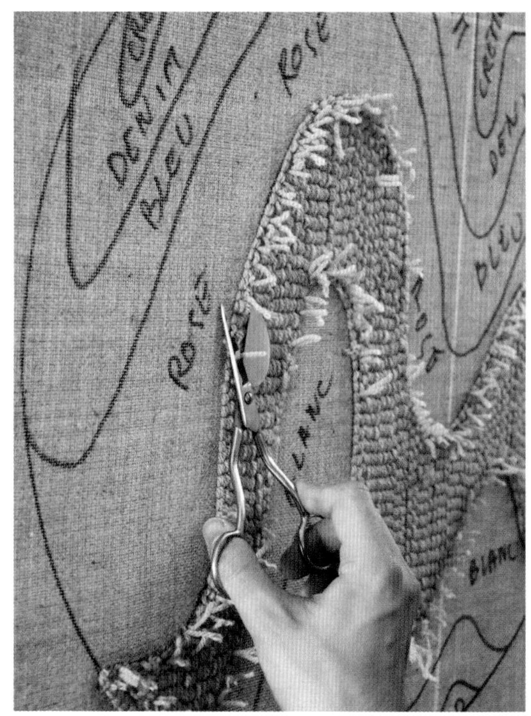

5 Fill in the shape by drawing vertical lines (from bottom to top) side by side, leaving a very slight space between them.

6 On the back of the piece, remove any protruding strands by cutting them with regular or duckbill scissors, or by pulling on them lightly.

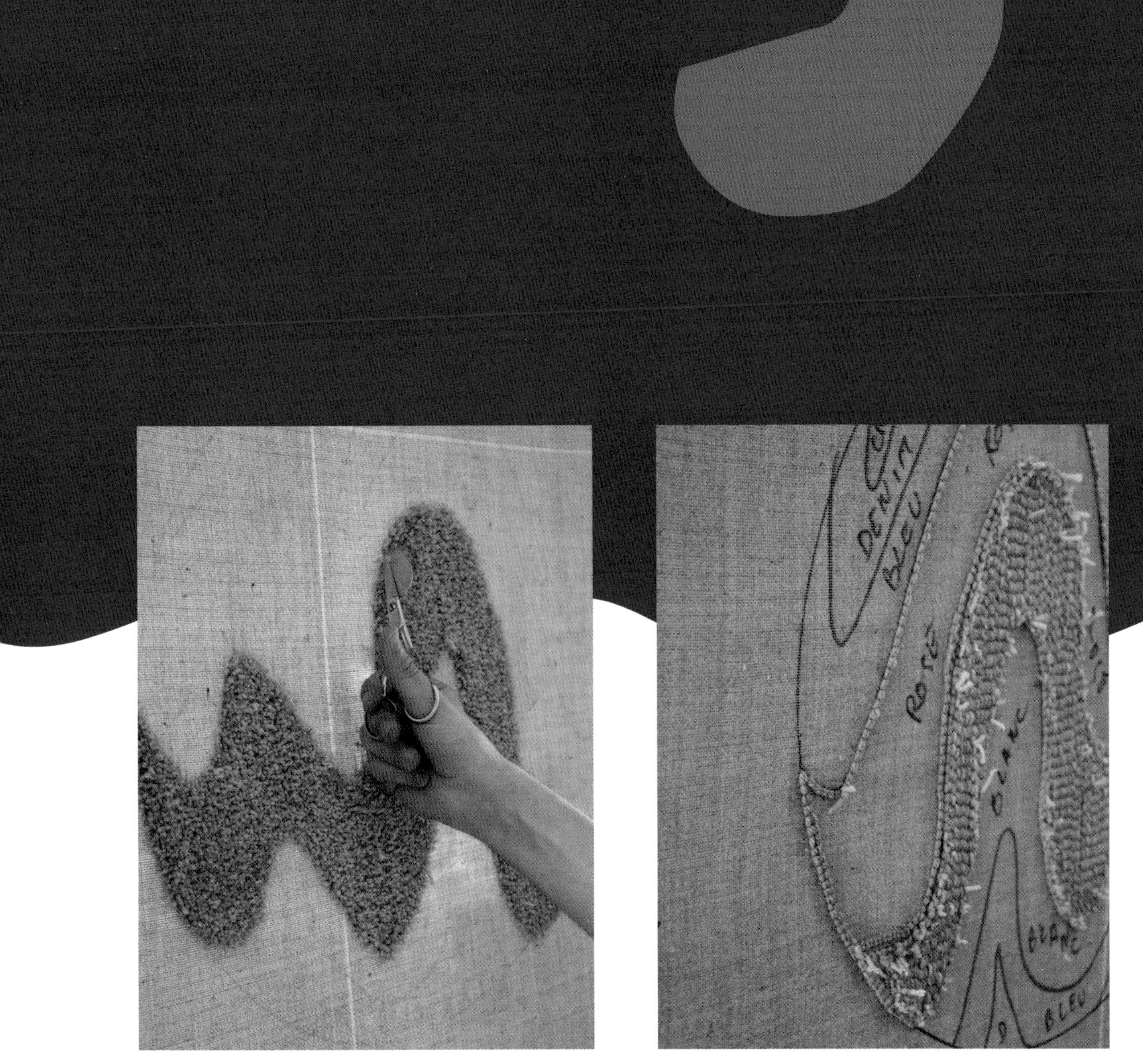

7 On the front side of the frame, trim and clean up the shape using regular or duckbill scissors.

8 Repeat steps 4 to 7 for the salmon shape and continue in the same manner until all shapes have been tufted.

9 For how to proceed with the rest of the steps to finish this project, follow the instructions on pages 46 to 56 of the "Technical Guide." This rug was used as the example for all the explanations.

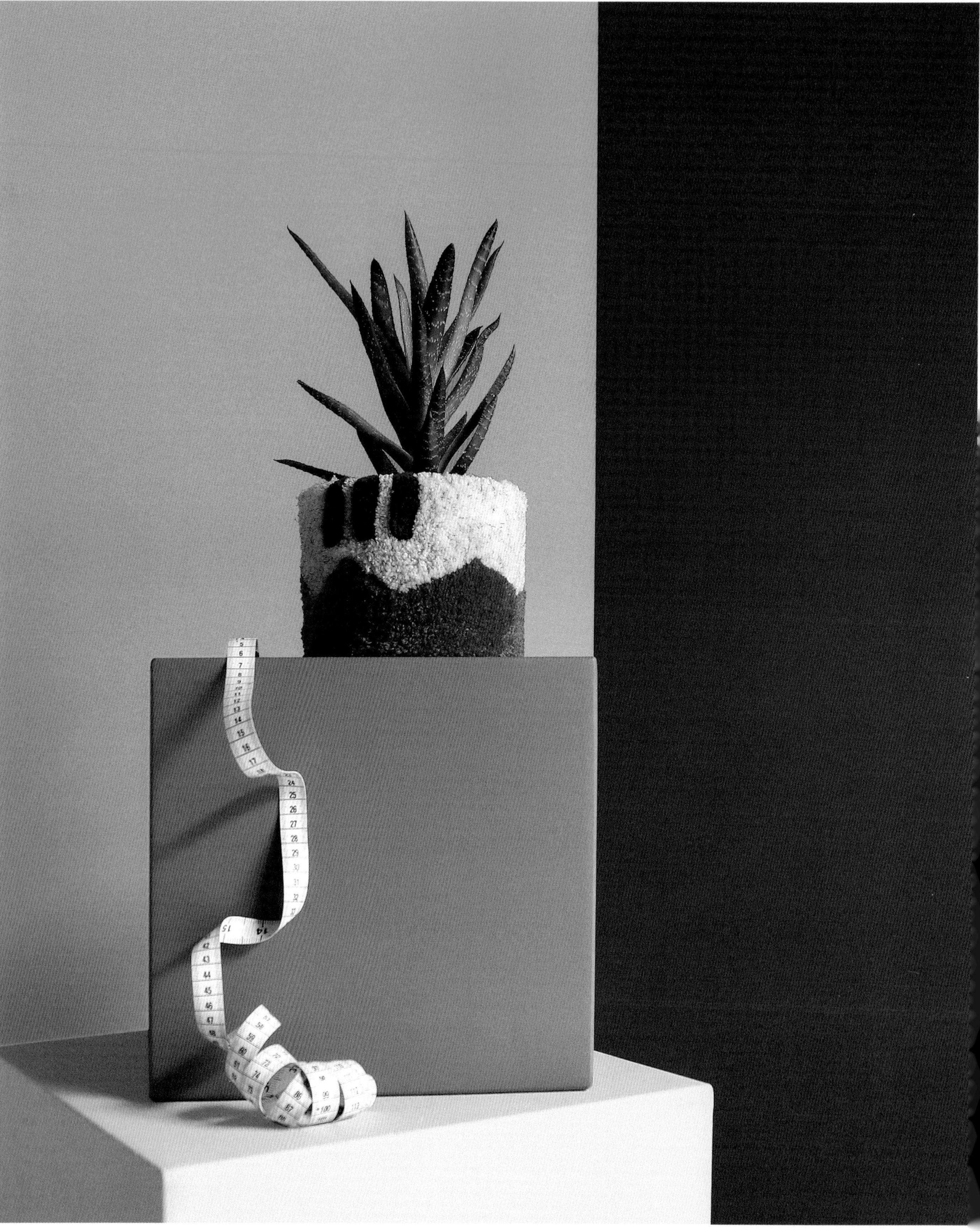

Difficulty * Dimensions: 17 × 4 7/10 in. (43 × 12 cm)
Diameter: 5 in. (13 cm)

PLANTER COVER

Materials

- Basic materials (pages 8 to 17)
- Your choice of plant pot (pot shown in photos is 5 in./13 cm tall)
- Felt ⅛ in. (3 mm) thick, 17 7/10 × 27½ in. (45 × 70 cm) or size needed to fit your pot (see step 2 on page 72)
- Glue gun and glue stick or tube of fast-setting fabric glue
- Tape measure

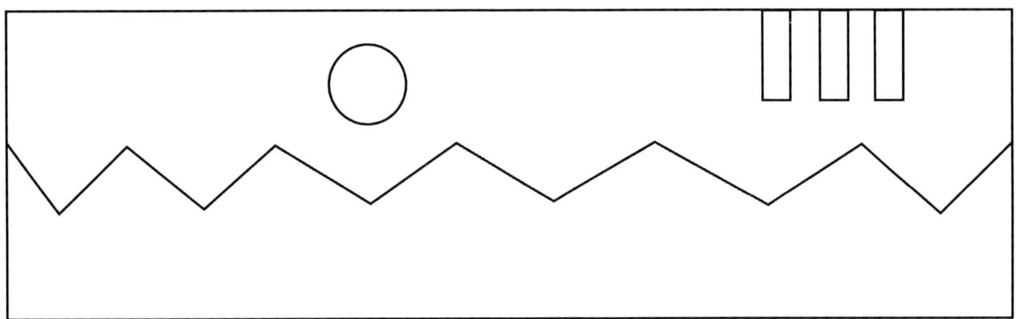

Yarn

Color	Yarn Brand	Weight of Yarn Ball	Qty.	No. of 3.5 oz. (100 g) Double Yarn Balls Needed	Actual Qty. Used
#911 NATURAL	DMC Merino Essential 4 Tweed	1.8 oz. (50 g)	2	1	2.7 oz. (75 g)
#979 ELECTRIC BLUE	DMC Knitty 4	1.8 oz. (50 g)	2	1	0.35 oz. (10 g)
#766 GOLD	DMC Knitty 4	1.8 oz. (50 g)	2	1	2.1 oz. (60 g)
#77 SALMON	Katia Merino Baby	1.8 oz. (50 g)	2	1	0.6 oz. (17 g)

1 To determine the size of the design to be tufted, use a tape measure to determine the circumference and height of the pot. Then add 1 in. (2 cm) to the circumference (with this length, the pot will fit more easily). For my pot, the circumference measures 16 + 1 in. (41 + 2 cm) and the height is 5 in. (12 cm). My design therefore measures 17 × 5 in. (43 × 12 cm).

2 On the felt, draw a rectangle that is 1½ in. (4 cm) longer than the design (18½ in. [47 cm]), and the height is the same. Cut it with regular scissors.

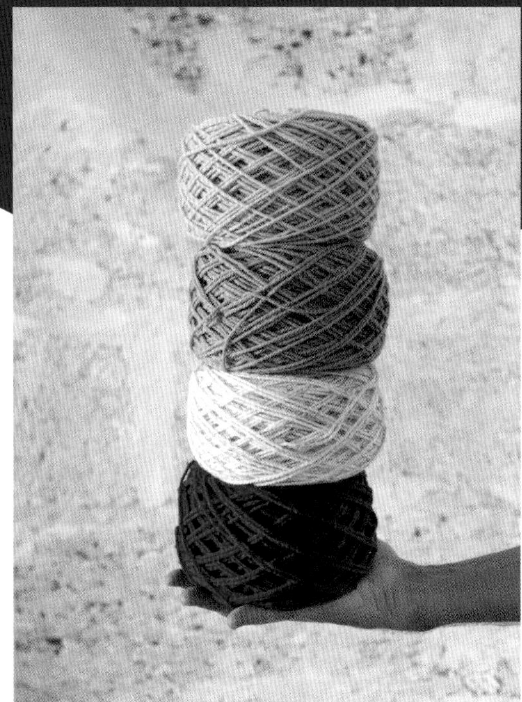

3 On the primary cloth stretched over the frame, draw a 17 × 5 in. (43 × 12 cm) rectangle using a marker (see step 1).

4 Copy the design and indicate the colors.

5 Make the double yarn balls needed per the table on page 71.

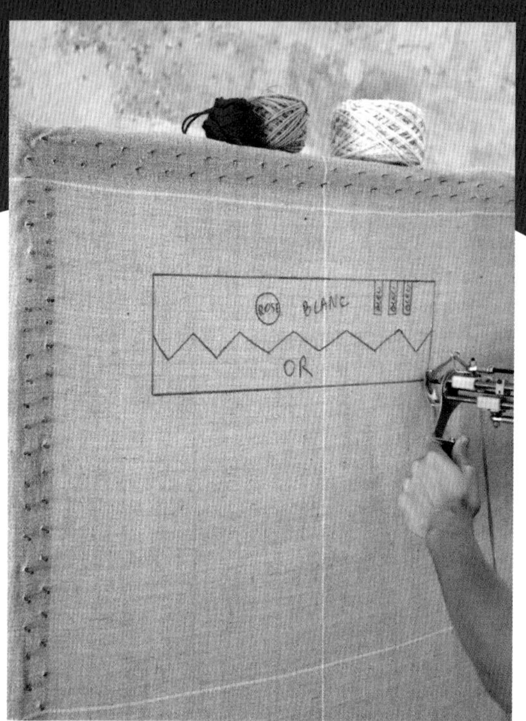

6 Start by tufting the outlines of the gold-colored shape, then fill it in by drawing vertical lines (from bottom to top) side by side, leaving a very slight space between them.

7 On the front side of the frame, trim and clean up the shape using regular or duckbill scissors.

8 Repeat steps 6 and 7 for the salmon and blue shapes.

9 Finish by tufting the natural color. There's no need to trim the edges at this stage. On the back of the piece, remove any protruding strands by trimming with regular or duckbill scissors, or pulling on them lightly.

10 Using regular scissors, cut out the tufted piece, leaving a 1½-in. border (4 cm) all the way around.

11 Notch the four corners of the piece, as shown in the photo.

12 Using the carpet and flexible flooring glue and the flat brush, glue the edges of the tufting cloth, fold them over, and cover them again with glue.

13 Spread glue over the entire back of the piece.

14 Gently apply the felt to the glued area (leaving 1½ in. (4 cm) of unglued felt on one end). Let dry for a few hours.

15 Once the glue has dried, turn the piece over and brush it with a wire brush.

16 Move on to shearing to smooth out the surface. Trim the shapes if necessary.

17 Using the glue gun or tube of fabric glue, apply glue to the remaining 1½ in. (4 cm) of felt.

18 Before the glue dries, quickly form a cylinder and glue the piece, overlapping this extra felt on the inside.

19 Apply pressure with your fingers until the hot glue has cooled. If you're using fabric glue, follow the instructions on the packaging.

20 Place the potted plant inside the planter cover!

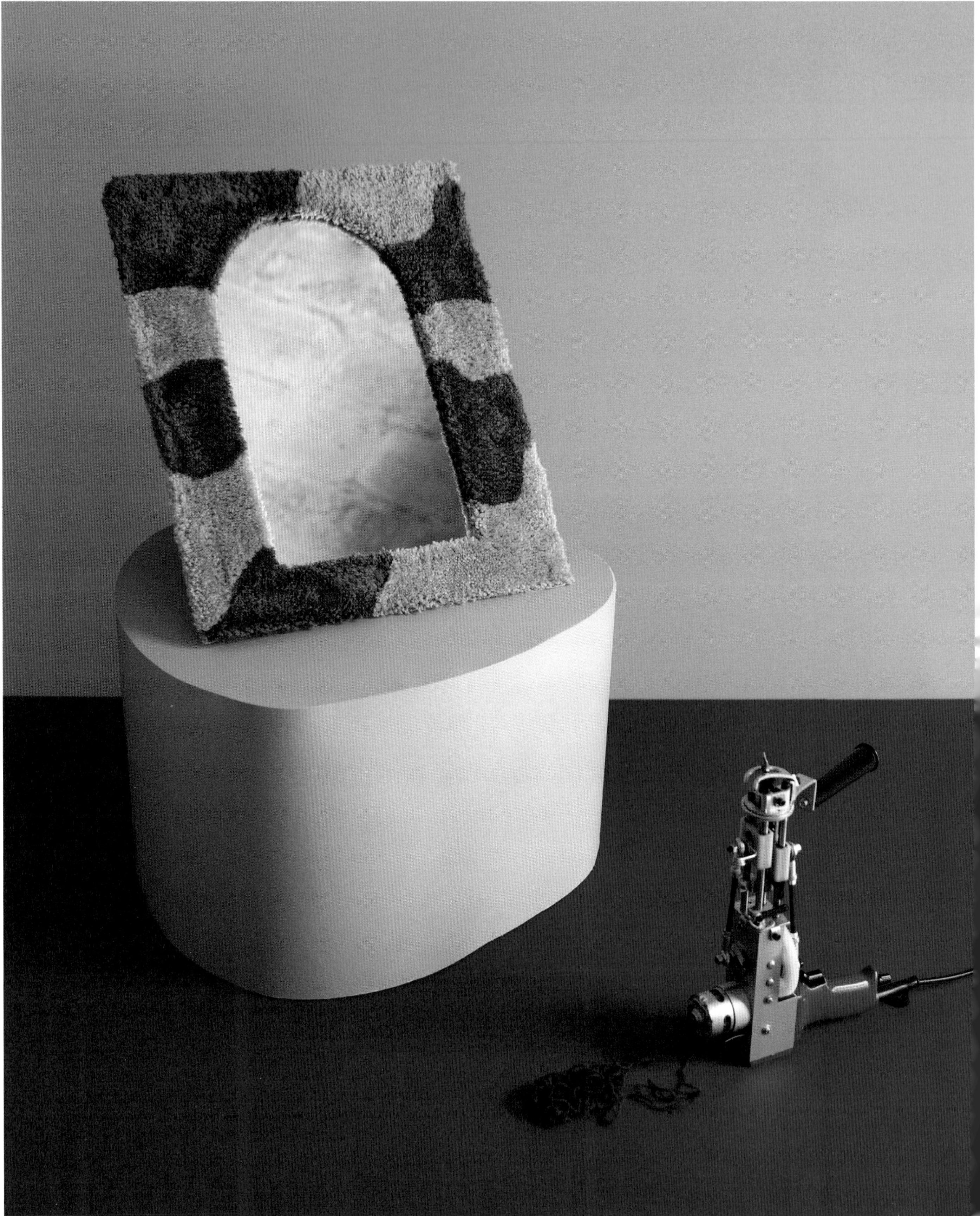

Difficulty ** Dimensions: 16 × 20 in. (40 × 50 cm)

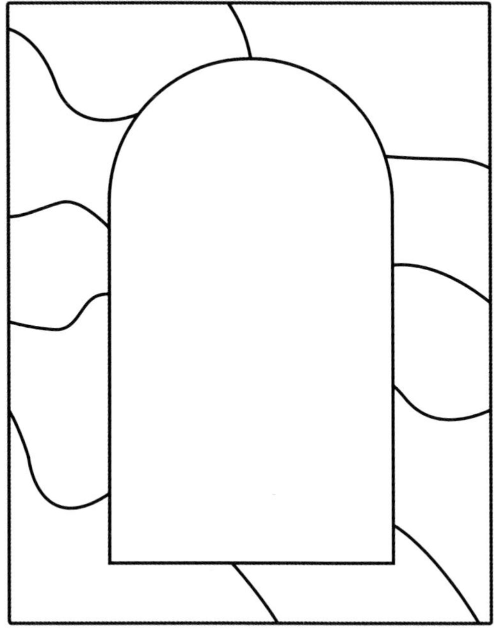

Materials

- Basic materials (pages 8 to 17)
- MDF board, ⅛ in. (3 mm) thick, 16 × 20 in. (40 × 50 cm)
- Mirror, ⅛ in. (3 mm) thick, 12 × 18 in. (30 × 45 cm)
- Secondary backing fabric 8.9 oz. per yd. sq. (300 g per sq. m), 16 × 20 in. (40 × 50 cm)
- Liquid transparent glue for paper and cardboard
- Flat brush ¾ in. (2 cm) wide

Yarn

Color	Yarn Brand	Weight of Yarn Ball	Qty.	No. of 3.5 oz. (100 g) Double Yarn Balls Needed	Actual Qty. Used
#26 DARK GREEN	Katia Merino Baby	1.8 oz. (50 g)	2	1	1.4 oz. (40 g)
#964 SAND	DMC Knitty 4	1.8 oz. (50 g)	2	1	1.4 oz. (40 g)

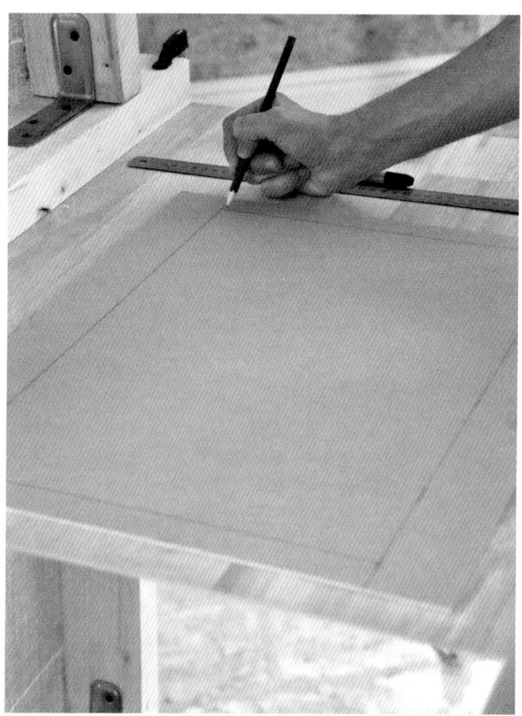

1 Place the mirror in the center of the MDF board. Using a marker or pencil, draw around the edge of the mirror. Also draw the extra 2 in. (5 cm) borders on the long sides and 1 in. (2.5 cm) borders on the short sides.

2 Using the flat brush, spread liquid glue on the back of the mirror and on the rectangle drawn on the MDF board.

3 Carefully place the mirror on the MDF board, pressing on it lightly, and let dry overnight.

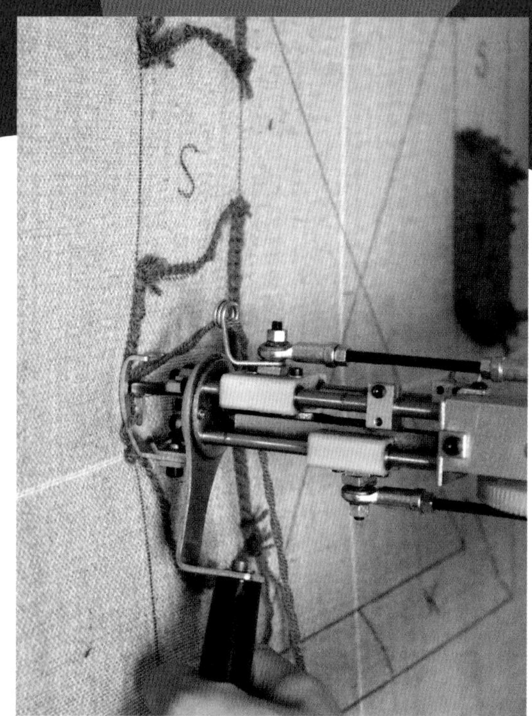

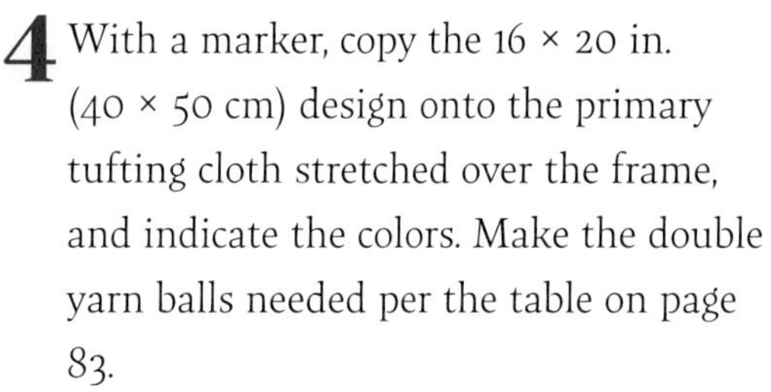

4 With a marker, copy the 16 × 20 in. (40 × 50 cm) design onto the primary tufting cloth stretched over the frame, and indicate the colors. Make the double yarn balls needed per the table on page 83.

5 Start by tufting the outlines of the dark green shapes, then fill them in by drawing vertical lines (from bottom to top) side by side, leaving a very slight space between them.

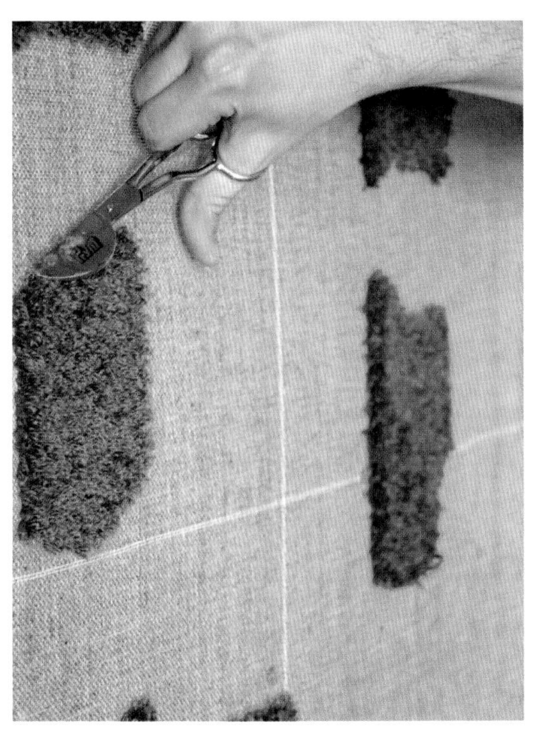

6 On the front side of the frame, trim and clean up the shapes using regular or duckbill scissors.

7 Finish by tufting the sand color. On the back of the piece, remove any protruding strands by trimming them with regular or duckbill scissors, or by pulling on them lightly.

8 Using a putty knife or disposable glove, cover the surface with carpet and flexible flooring glue, leaving a ½ in. (1.5 cm) inner edge with no glue.

9 Using a trowel, apply the secondary backing fabric to the glue. Let dry for 12 hours.

NOTE

The frame may be laid down horizontally during gluing, if desired.

10 Once the glue has dried, cut off the excess cloth using regular scissors to reveal the unglued edge.

11 Using regular scissors, cut the tufting cloth around the piece, leaving a ¾-in. (2-cm) border.

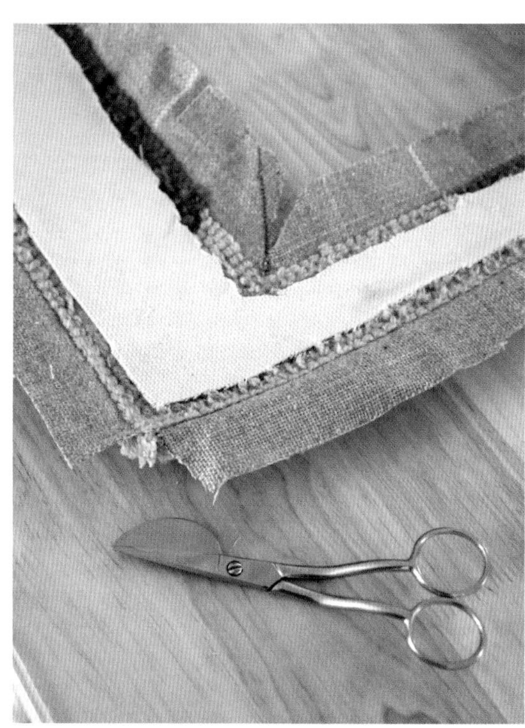

12 Using regular or duckbill scissors, cut the primary cloth at the center of the design, leaving a ¾-in. (2-cm) border. Cut notches every 1½ in. (4 cm).

13 Notch the four outer corners of the piece, as shown in the photo.

14 Apply carpet and flexible flooring glue to the primary cloth using the flat brush.

15 Fold over the primary cloth onto the back and cover the entire surface with glue.

16 Carefully place the MDF board on the back.

17 Turn it over and make sure the shape of the frame fits snugly with the edges of the board. Readjust if necessary. Let dry overnight.

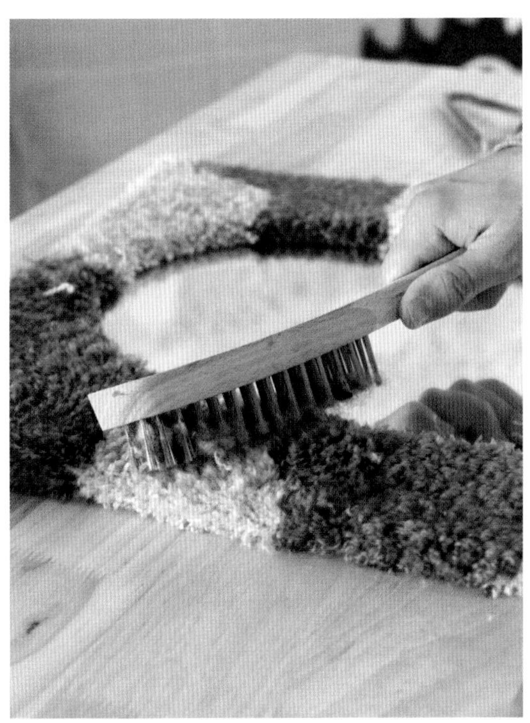

18 Once the glue is dry, turn the piece over and brush it with a wire brush.

19 Move on to shearing to smooth out the surface. Trim outlines of the shapes and edges, if necessary.

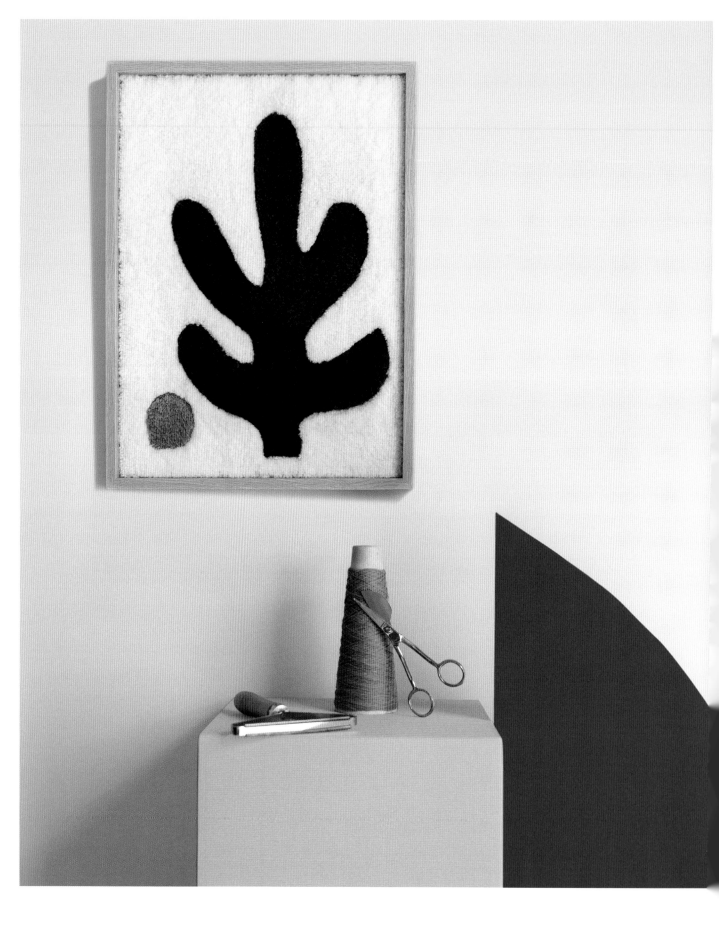

Difficulty ** Dimensions: 12 × 16 in. (30 × 40 cm) (without frame)

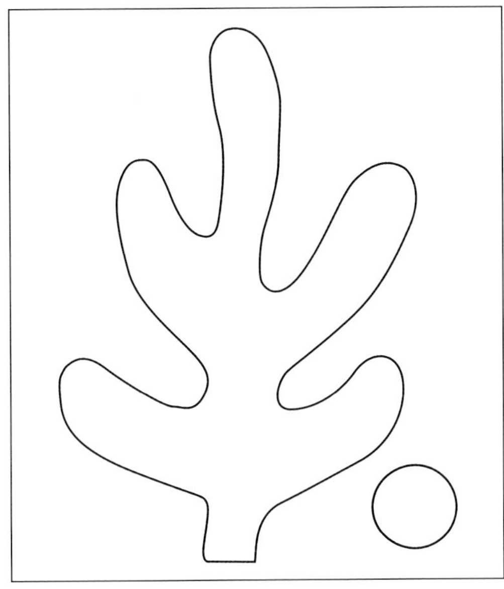

Materials

- Basic materials (pages 8 to 17)
- Secondary backing fabric 4.4 oz. per sq. yd. (150 g per sq. m), 12 × 16 in. (30 × 40 cm)
- Wood photo frame, 12 × 16 in. (30 × 40 cm) (frame in photos is 1 in. [2.5 cm] thick)
- Liquid transparent glue for paper and cardboard
- Small offset spatula or flat artist's brush to spread the glue
- Triangle ruler
- A large book (that will be used as a weight)

Yarn

Color	Yarn Brand	Weight of Yarn Ball	Qty.	No. of 3.5 oz. (100 g) Double Yarn Balls Needed	Actual Qty. Used
#961 WHITE	DMC Knitty 4	1.8 oz. (50 g)	2	1	3.5 oz. (100 g)
#979 ELECTRIC BLUE	DMC Knitty 4	1.8 oz. (50 g)	2	1	1.9 oz. (55 g)
#77 SALMON	Katia Merino Baby	1.8 oz. (50 g)	2	1	0.6 oz. (17 g)

1 With a marker, draw a 12 × 16 in. (30 × 40 cm) rectangle on the cloth stretched onto the frame, using the back of the photo frame as a template. Copy the design and indicate the colors.

2 Make the double yarn balls needed per the table on page 95.

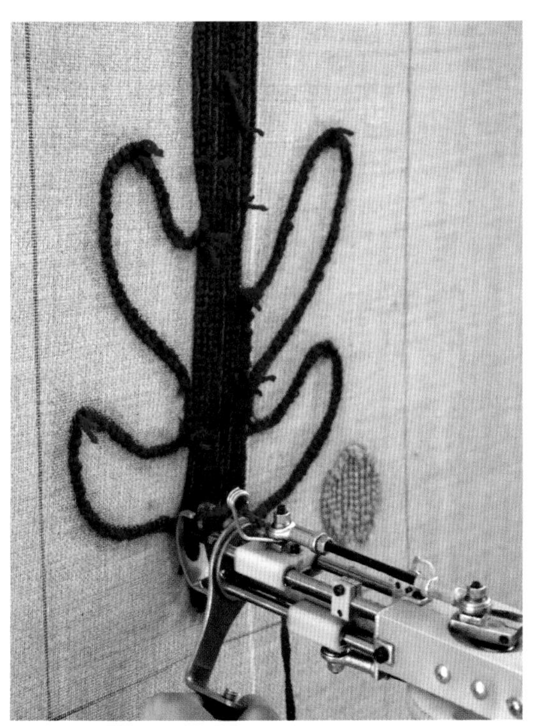

3 Start by tufting the small circle and then the blue leaf. Fill them in by drawing vertical lines (from bottom to top) side by side, leaving a very slight space between lines.

4 On the front side of the frame, trim and clean up the shapes using regular or duckbill scissors.

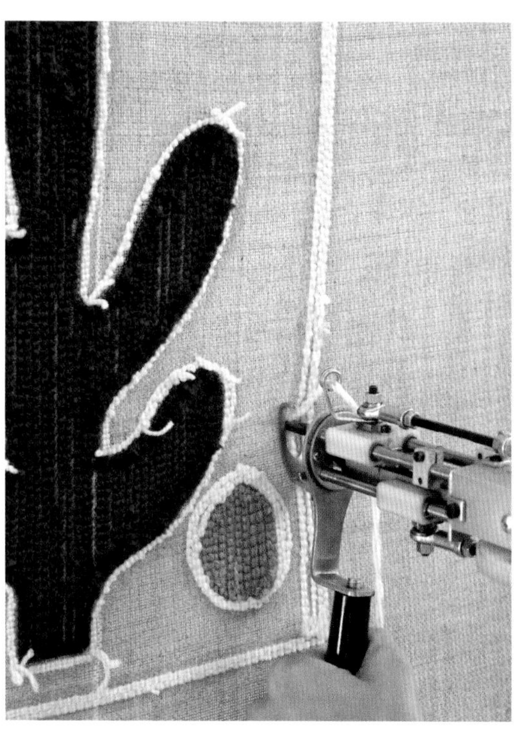

5 Tuft the outline of the rectangle, then fill the shape, always in vertical lines and from bottom to top.

6 On the back of the piece, remove any protruding strands by trimming them with regular or duckbill scissors, or by pulling on them lightly.

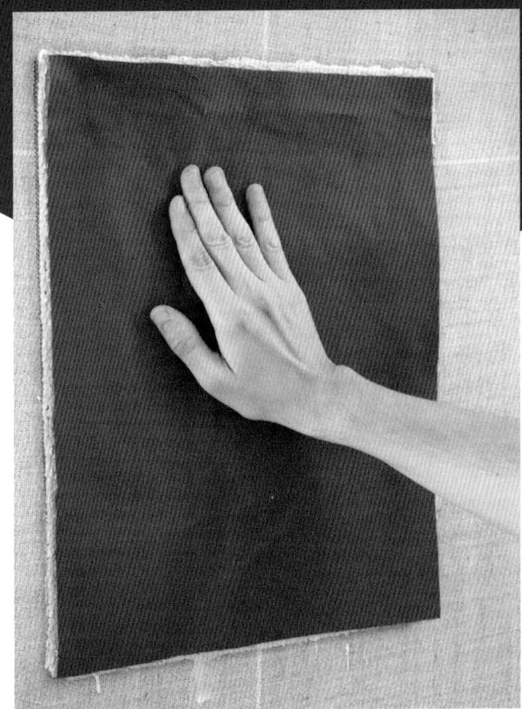

7 Using a putty knife or disposable glove, cover the entire surface with carpet and flexible flooring glue.

8 With the help of a trowel, apply the backing fabric to the glue. Let dry for 12 hours.

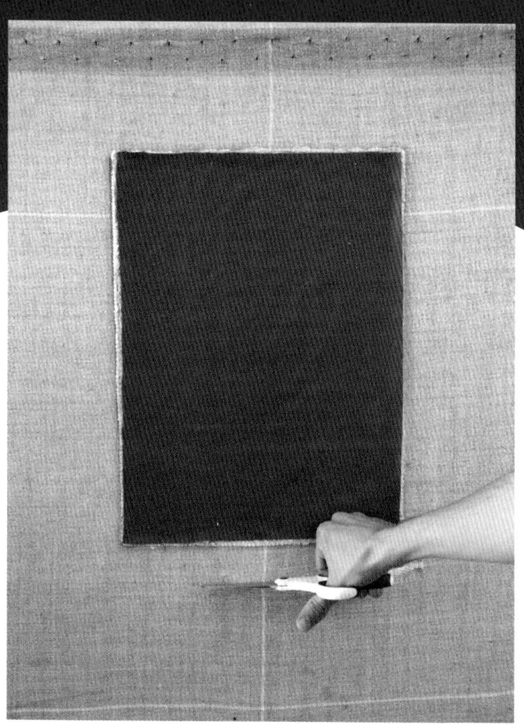

9 Once the glue has dried, cut the primary tufting cloth all around the piece, leaving a 2-in. (5-cm) border.

10 Turn the piece over and brush with a wire brush.

11 Move on to the shearing stage to smooth out the surface. Trim shapes, if necessary.

12 Using a spatula, apply a thin layer of liquid glue to the back of the frame.

TIP

Place a large book on the front of the piece during the drying process to weigh it down and prevent the bottom from warping from the moisture in the glue.

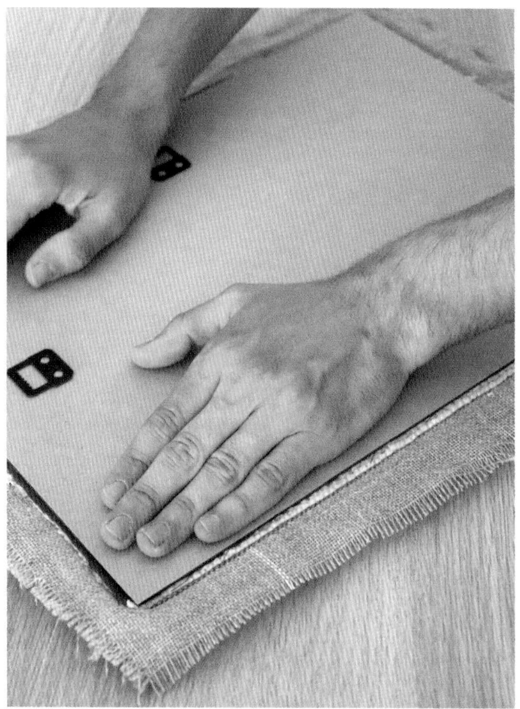

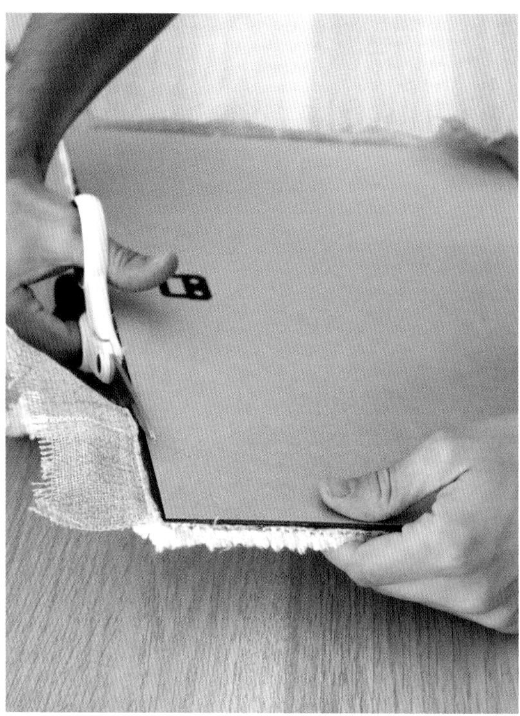

13 Turn the tufted piece over and apply the pre-glued backing. Press with the flat of your hand to help the glue adhere to the fabric. Let dry for 4 hours.

14 Using regular scissors, trim off the excess primary fabric, shaving the sides of the back.

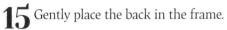

15 Gently place the back in the frame.

16 Use the tip of the triangle ruler to tuck in any yarn that may be protruding.

17 Turn the frame over. Use one side of the triangle ruler to tuck in any last strands.

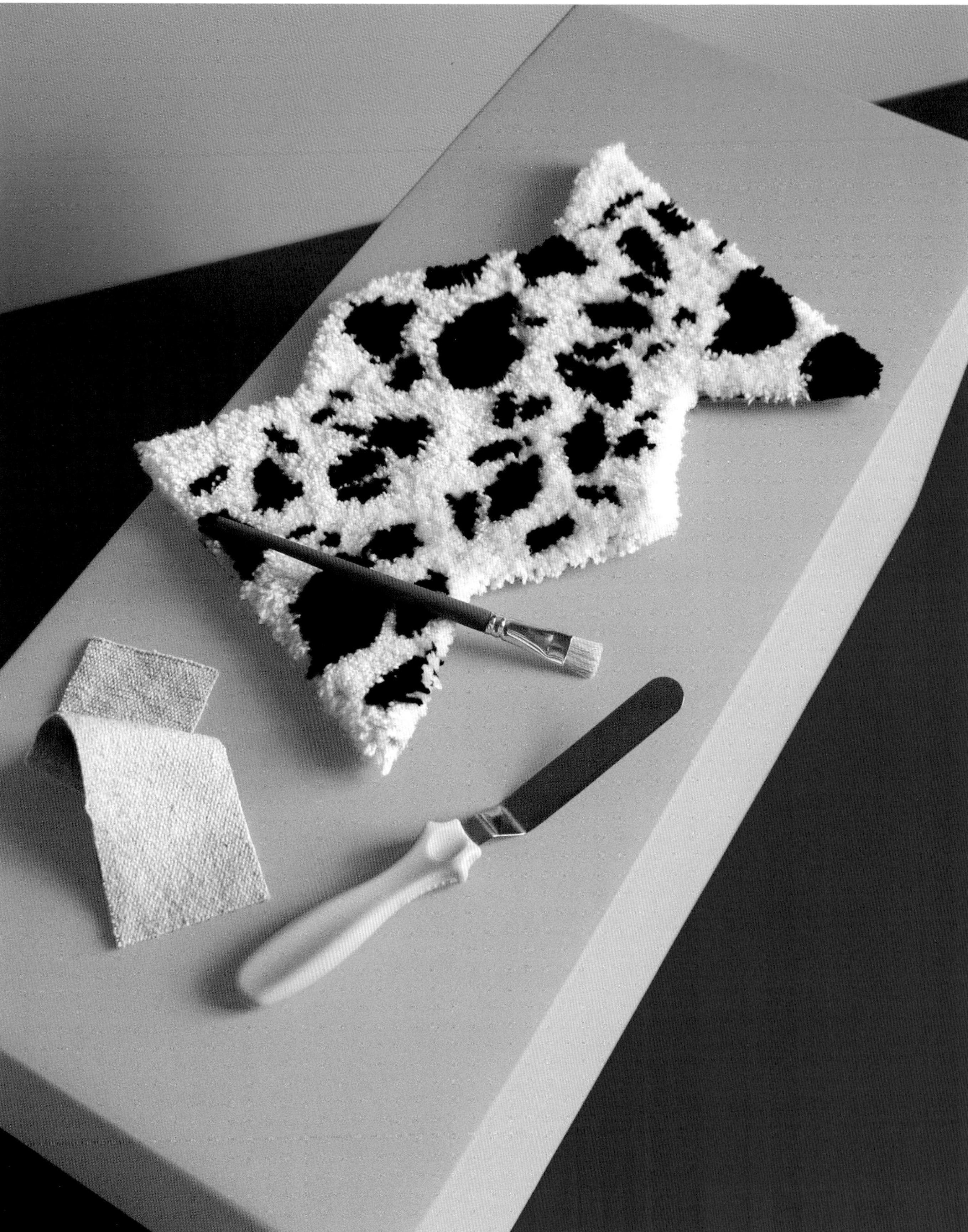

Difficulty * Dimensions: 12½ × 8¼ in. (32 × 21 cm)

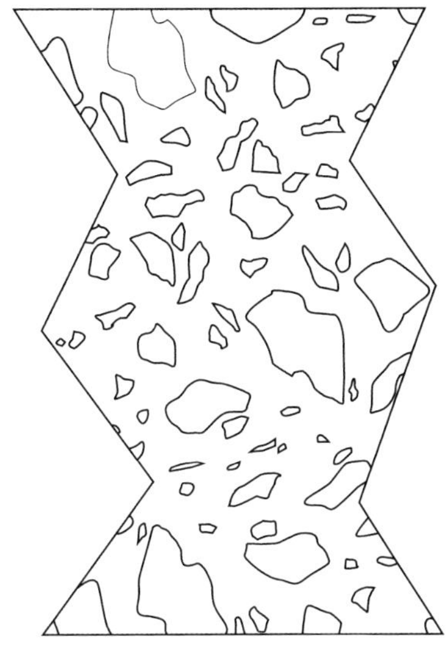

Materials

- Basic materials (pages 8 to 17)
- Felt ⅛ in. (3 mm) thick, 17⁷⁄₁₀ × 27½ in. (45 × 70 cm)

Yarn

Color	Yarn Brand	Weight of Yarn Ball	Qty.	No. of 3.5 oz. (100 g) Double Yarn Balls Needed	Actual Qty. Used
#961 WHITE	DMC Knitty 4	1.8 oz. (50 g)	2	1	0.9 oz. (25 g)
#965 BLACK	DMC Knitty 4	1.8 oz. (50 g)	2	1	1.6 oz. (45 g)

1 With a marker, copy the design onto the primary cloth stretched on the frame, in a 12½ × 8¼ in. (32 × 21 cm) area, and indicate the colors.

2 Make the double yarn balls needed per the table on page 105.

3 Start by outlining the black shapes, then fill them in by drawing vertical lines (from bottom to top) side by side, leaving a very slight space between them.

4 On the front side of the frame, trim and clean the shapes using regular or duckbill scissors.

5 Tuft the outline of the rug in white, then fill in the shape with vertical lines from bottom to top.

6 On the back of the piece, remove any protruding strands by trimming them with classic or duckbill scissors, or by pulling on them lightly.

7 Using regular scissors, cut the primary tufting cloth all around the piece, leaving a 1½-in. (4-cm) border.

8 Draw and cut out a 13¼ × 9 in. (34 × 23 cm) rectangle from the felt (¾ in. [2 cm] larger than the tufted piece).

9 Cut down the primary cloth border to half the width. Clip all points.

10 Using a flat brush and the carpet and flexible flooring adhesive, glue the edges of the primary cloth and fold over.

11 Cover the entire surface with glue.

12 Place the felt over it and apply pressure to the entire surface for better adhesion. Let it dry overnight.

13 Once the glue has dried, trim off the excess felt using large scissors.

14 Trim the edges cleanly so that they are straight. When the rug is turned over, the felt should not be visible.

15 Turn the piece over and brush with a wire brush.

16 Move on to shearing to smooth out the surface. Trim shapes, if necessary.

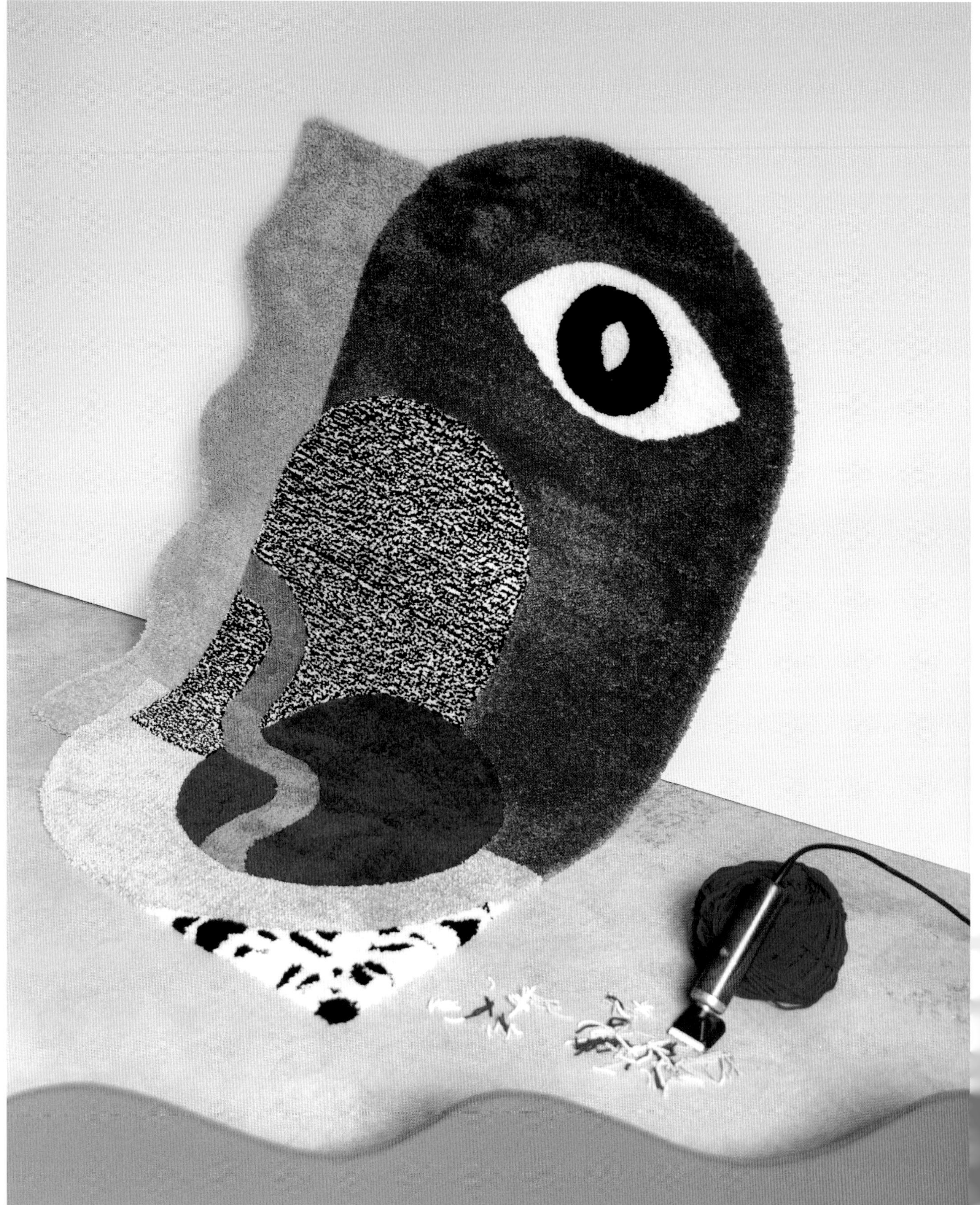

Difficulty * Dimensions: 47 × 30 in. (120 × 75 cm)**

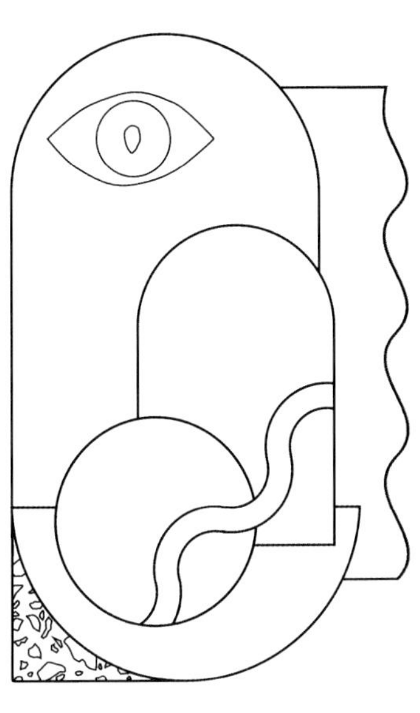

Materials

- Basic materials (pages 8 to 17)
- Large floor frame (here, 94½ × 63 in. [240 × 160 cm], with a center board that can be moved to fit the desired size)
- Secondary backing fabric 8.9 oz. per sq. yd. (300 g per sq. m), 51 × 31½ in. (130 × 80 cm)
- Rug binding tape (all slightly larger than 2 in./5 cm), 3 strips: 35 in. (88 cm), 40 in. (100 cm) and 74 in. (188 cm)

NOTE

To tuft the rug horizontally, I adjusted the frame's supports to leave a 55-in. (140-cm) space.

Yarn

Color	Yarn Brand	Weight of Yarn Ball	Qty.	No. of 3.5 oz. (100 g) Double Yarn Balls Needed	Actual Qty. Used
#961 WHITE	DMC Knitty 4	1.8 oz. (50 g)	2	1	2.8 oz. (80 g)
#979 ELECTRIC BLUE	DMC Knitty 4	1.8 oz. (50 g)	2	1	3.5 oz. (100 g)
#26 DARK GREEN	Katia Merino Baby	1.8 oz. (50 g)	8	4	14.1 oz. (400 g)
#66 LIGHT MAUVE	Katia Merino Baby	1.8 oz. (50 g)	2	1	3.5 oz. (100 g)
#965 BLACK #961 WHITE	DMC Knitty 4	1.8 oz. (50 g) each	1 each	1	3.5 oz. (100 g)
#965 BLACK	DMC Knitty 4	1.8 oz. (50 g)	2	1	1.6 oz. (45 g)
#766 GOLD	DMC Knitty 4	1.8 oz. (50 g)	2	1	1.8 oz. (50 g)
#77 SALMON	Katia Merino Baby	1.8 oz. (50 g)	4	2	7.1 oz. (200 g)

1 With a marker, copy the design onto the primary cloth stretched on the frame, in a 47 × 30 in. (120 × 75 cm) area, and indicate the colors.

2 Make the double yarn balls needed per the table on page 115. For the speckled part, wind one white and one black yarn together.

3 Tuft the shapes one after the other. Always start with the outline of the shape before filling it, drawing vertical lines (from bottom to top) side by side, leaving a very slight space between them.

4 On the front side of the frame, trim and clean up the shapes using regular or duckbill scissors. On the back of the piece, remove any protruding strands by trimming them with regular or duckbill scissors, or by pulling on them lightly.

TIP

If you're gluing vertically, tape the backing fabric at the corners to prevent it from falling off.

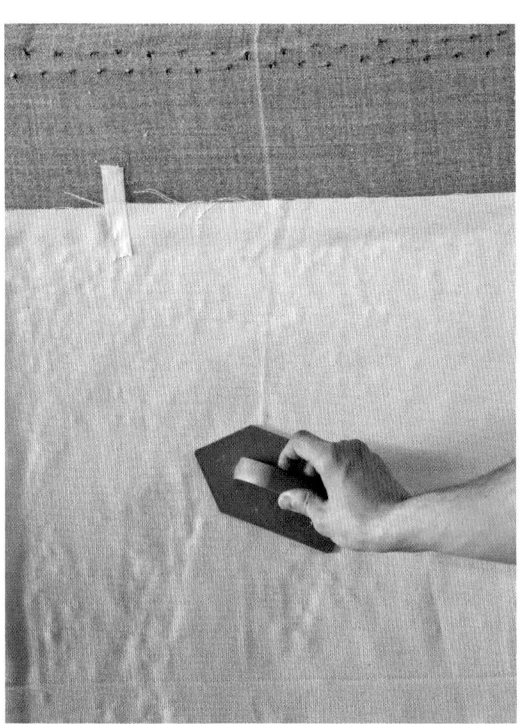

5 Using a putty knife or disposable glove, coat the surface with carpet and flexible flooring glue, leaving a ½-in. (1.5-cm) border.

6 Using a trowel, apply the secondary fabric to the glue. Let dry for 12 hours. Once the glue has dried, cut off the excess cloth with regular scissors, revealing the unglued edge.

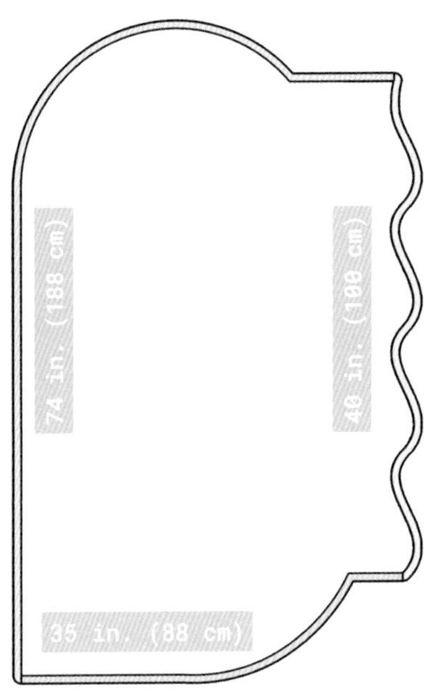

7 Using regular scissors, cut the primary tufting cloth all around the piece, leaving a ¾-in. (2-cm) border. Cut notches every 2 in. (5 cm) on the rounded parts of the design (the light mauve, dark green, and salmon shapes).

8 Apply glue to the rug binding tape and position the pieces as follows: the longest strip, 74 in. (188 cm), will run from the bottom left corner to the top right corner; the 40-in. (100-cm) strip will follow the wavy edge of the pink shape; the final 35-in. (88-cm) strip will fill the remaining bottom space.

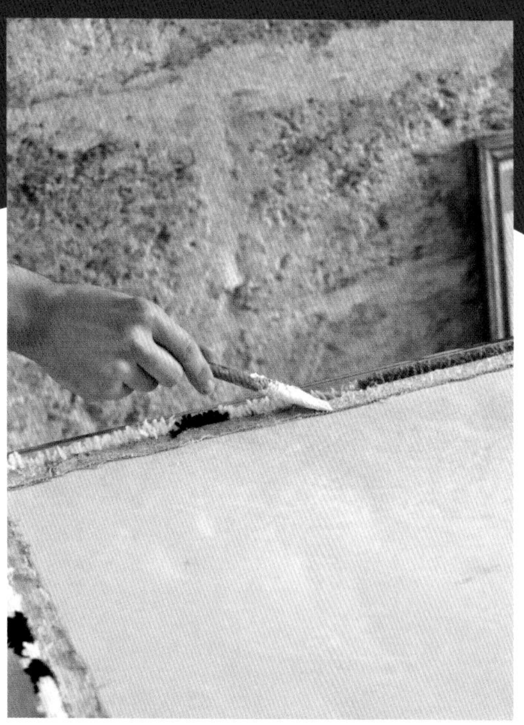

9 Fold and glue the tufting cloth using a flat brush.

10 For the salmon wavy shape, take the time to fit the binding tape to the shape. Once the strips are all applied, let dry for a few hours.

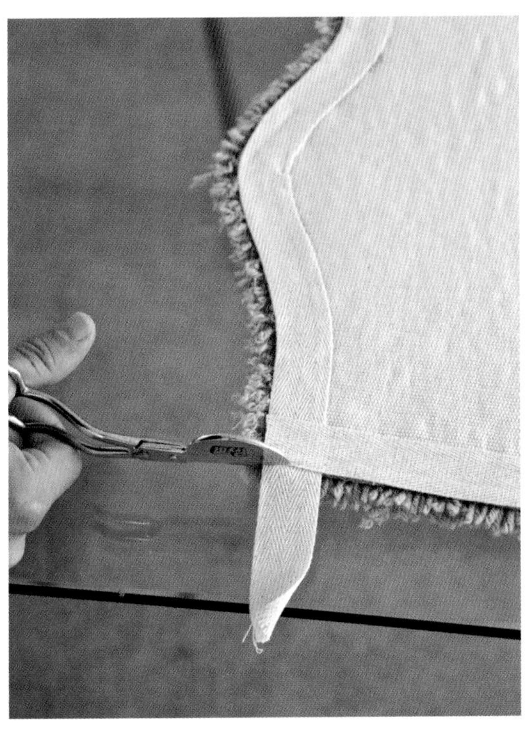

11 When the strips are dry, trim their ends using regular scissors.

12 Turn the piece over and brush with a wire brush.

13 Move on to shearing to smooth out the surface. Trim the shapes, if necessary.

14 To remove the last trimmed fibers, use the vacuum cleaner in brush mode.

TIP

This rug can be hung on the wall using simple, thin nails placed along its edges. The thickness of the rug will hide the nail heads.

Difficulty **   Dimensions: 12 × 16 in. (30 × 40 cm)

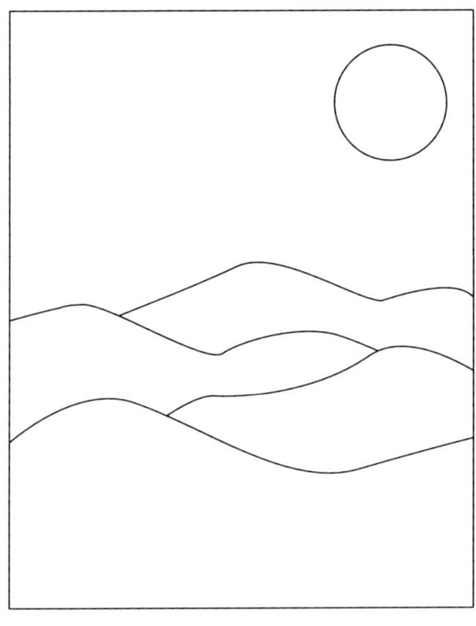

Materials

- Basic materials (pages 8 to 17)
- Secondary backing fabric 8.9 oz. per sq. yd. (300 g per sq. m), 11 × 15 in. (28 × 38 cm)
- Rug binding tape, 2 strips at 12½ in. (32 cm) and 2 strips at 16½ in. (42 cm)
- Dowel 12½ in. (32 cm) long, ½ in. (12 mm) in diameter. These are found in big box or home improvement stores for less than $1 for 18 to 24 in. (45.7 to 61 cm) and may have to be cut to size with a saw.
- Heavy-duty needle (with eye large enough for a strand of yarn)

Yarn

Color	Yarn Brand	Weight of Yarn Ball	Qty.	No. of 3.5 oz. (100 g) Double Yarn Balls Needed	Actual Qty. Used
CREAM	Pingouin Pingo First Doe	1.8 oz. (50 g)	2	1	1.4 oz. (40 g)
#66 LIGHT MAUVE	Katia Merino Baby	1.8 oz. (50 g)	2	1	0.5 oz. (15 g)
BROWN (NOISETTE)	Phildar Charly	1.8 oz. (50 g)	2	1	0.3 oz. (7 g)
#68 FAWN BROWN	Katia Basic Merino No.	1.8 oz. (50 g)	2	1	0.5 oz. (15 g)
#965 BLACK	DMC Knitty 4	1.8 oz. (50 g)	2	1	0.5 oz. (13 g)
#766 GOLD	DMC Knitty 4	1.8 oz. (50 g)	2	1	1.4 oz. (40 g)
#77 SALMON	Katia Merino Baby	1.8 oz. (50 g)	2	n/a	110.2 in. (280 cm)

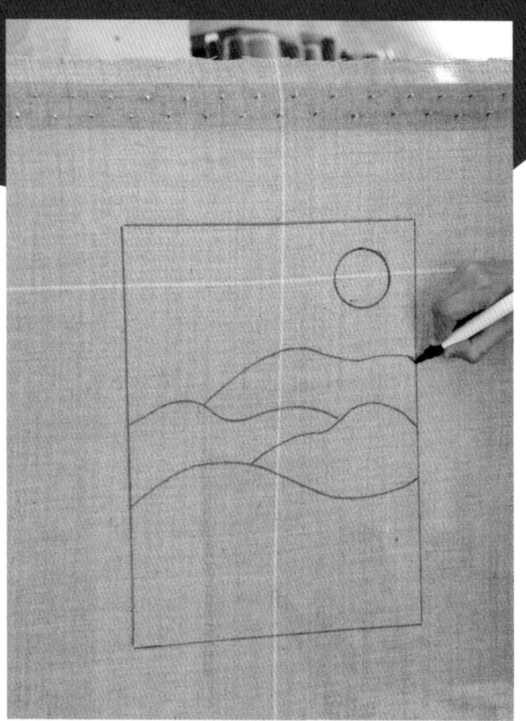

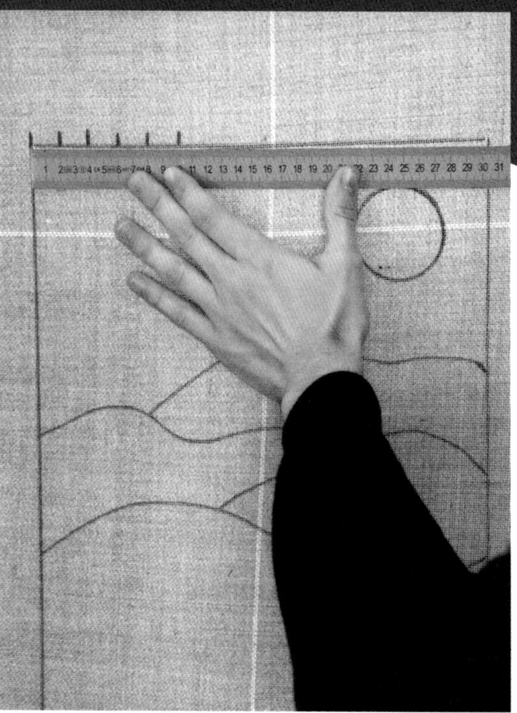

1 On the primary cloth stretched over the frame, draw a 12 × 16 in. (30 × 40 cm) rectangle with a marker and copy the design. Indicate the colors as well.

2 On the top, mark every ¾ in. (2 cm) with a large ruler (17 marks for 12 in. [16 marks for 30 cm]).

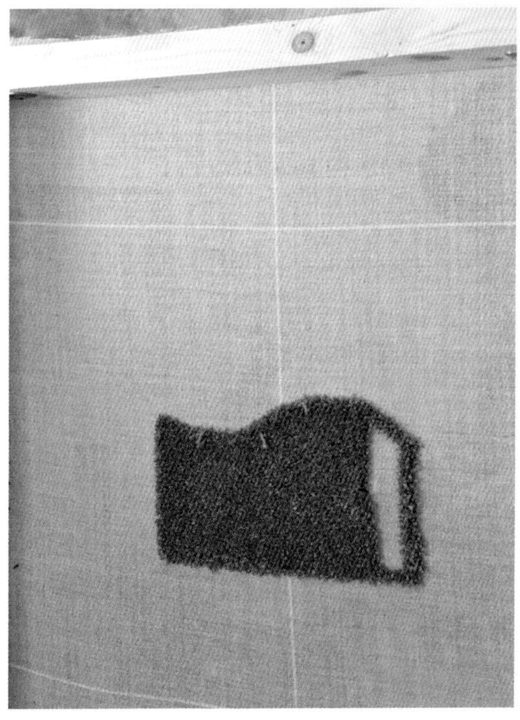

3 Make the double yarn balls needed per the table on page 125.

4 Start by tufting the outline of the gold-colored shape at the bottom, then fill it in by drawing vertical lines (from bottom to top) side by side, leaving a very slight space between them.

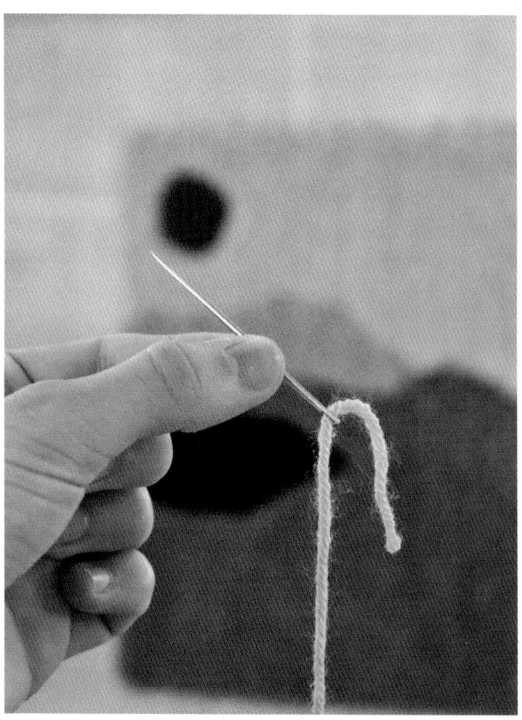

5 Continue with the other shapes. Before tufting a new one, don't forget to trim the outline of the finished shape on the front side of the frame. On the back of the piece, remove any protruding strands by cutting them off with regular or duckbill scissors, or by pulling on them lightly.

6 Insert the salmon yarn through the eye of the needle. You will need about 110 in. (280 cm) to make the loops around the dowel.

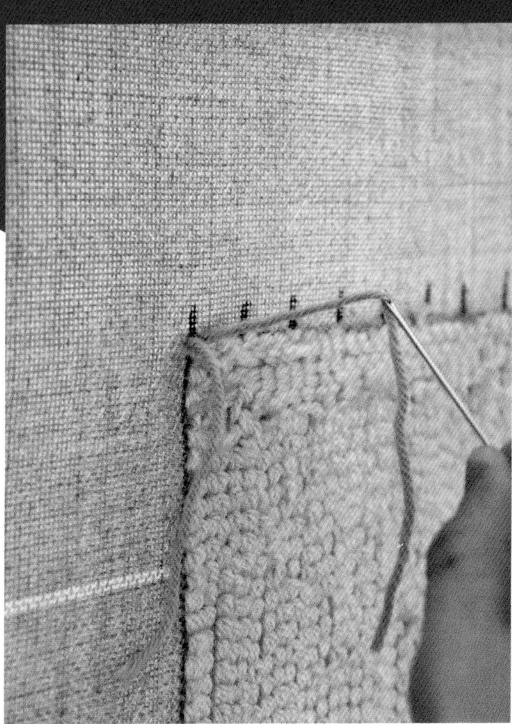

7 Insert the needle through the back side, at the first mark. Pull the yarn through on the front side, leaving a tail of about 4 in. (10 cm) on the back.

8 On the front, make a small stitch about ⅛ in. (2 mm), passing the needle and yarn through to the back.

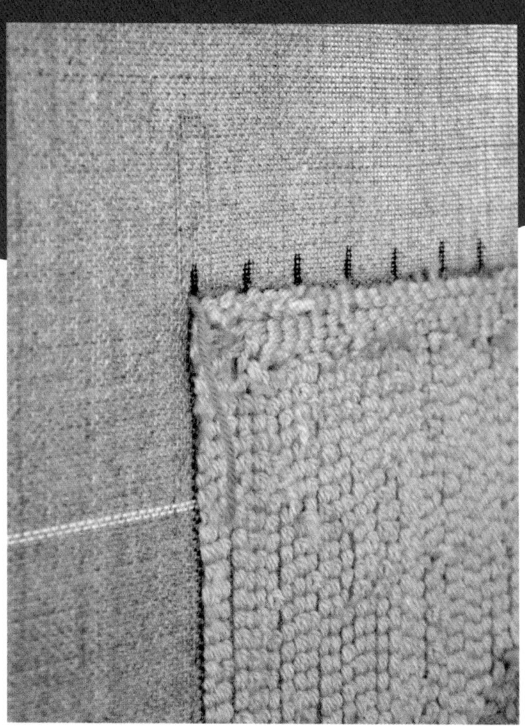

9 When you pull the yarn through, leave a loop of about 2 in. (5 cm) on the front side of the frame.

10 At the back of the frame, insert the needle at the second mark (¾ in. [2 cm] from the first one). Repeat steps 7 to 9 until you reach the last mark.

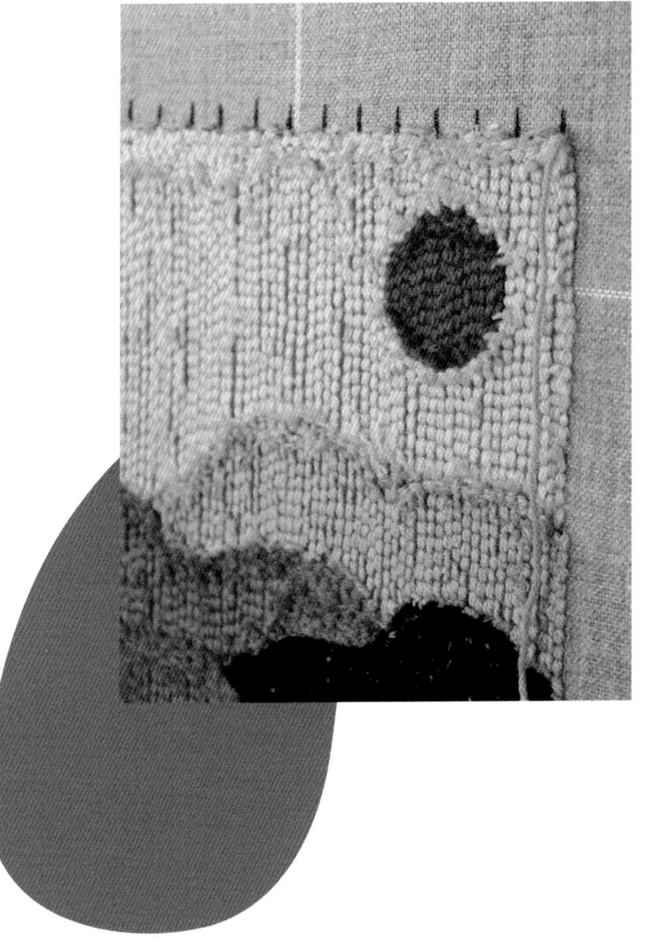

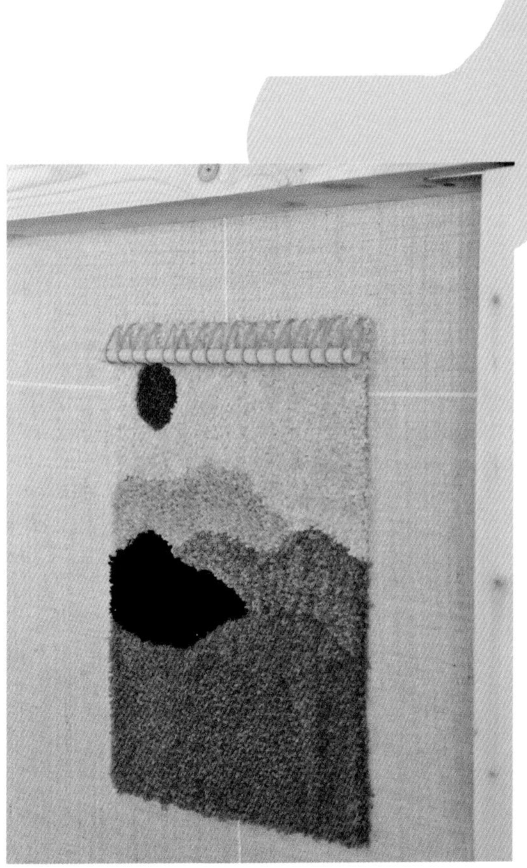

11 Place the dowel in the loops you just made. The piece should be straight when hung up. Adjust the yarn so that the dowel is level and not tilted.

12 For the gluing stage, work vertically or horizontally, laying the frame down. Using a putty knife or disposable glove, cover the surface with carpet and flexible flooring glue, leaving a border of ½ in. (1.5 cm) with no glue.

13 Using a trowel, apply the backing fabric to the glue. Let dry for 12 hours.

14 Once the glue has dried, use regular scissors to cut the primary cloth all around the piece, leaving a 4-in. (10-cm) border. On the back, tie a knot at the ends of the pink yarn. Double it if necessary (it needs to be large enough not to be pulled through to the other side). Trim excess yarn.

15 Cut the primary cloth border down to ¾ in. (2 cm).

16 Use the lighter trick to harden the cloth fibers around the edge (page 50).

17 Fold back and glue the primary cloth with a flat brush. For the corners of the cloth, fold over the edges, as shown in the photo.

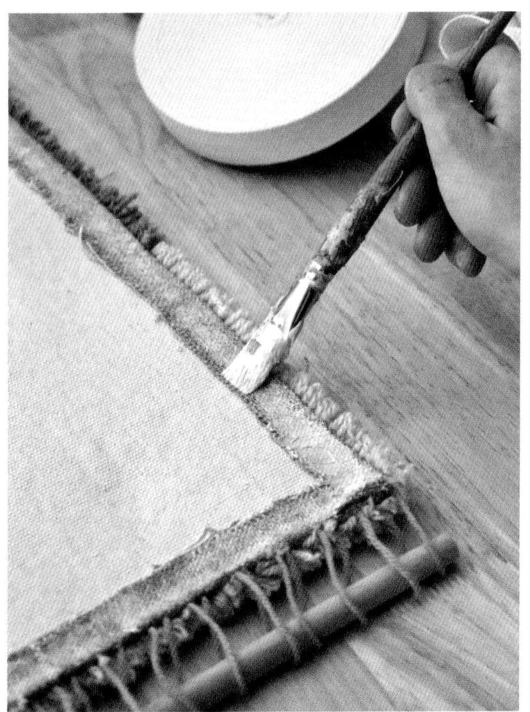

18 Apply glue to the binding tape and gently place the strips on the edges. Let dry for a few hours.

19 When the strips are dry, trim the ends using regular scissors.

20 Turn the piece over and brush with a wire brush.

21 Move on to shearing to smooth out the surface. Trim the shapes, if needed.

Difficulty * Dimensions: 16 × 24 in. (40 × 60 cm) (without fringe) 16 × 43 ½ in. (40 × 110 cm) (with fringe and dowel)**

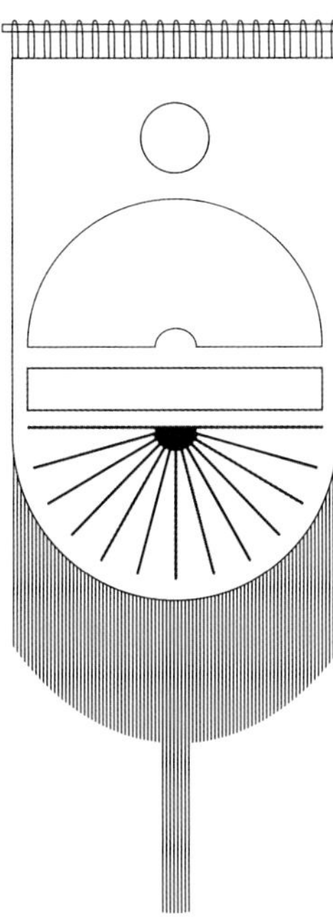

Materials

- Basic materials (pages 8 to 17)
- Secondary backing fabric 8.9 oz. per sq. yd. (300 g per sq. m), 17 × 25 in. (42 × 62 cm)
- Rug binding tape, 1 strip at 17 in. (42 cm) and 1 strip at 57 in. (145 cm)
- Dowel, 17 in. (42 cm) long, ½ in. (12 mm) in diameter. These are found in big box or home improvement stores for less than $1 for 18 to 24 in. and may have to be cut to size with a saw.
- Heavy-duty needle (with eye large enough for a strand of yarn)
- Mattress needle (large enough that many strands can be threaded on at the same time)
- Large, 1-yd. (1-m) ruler
- Comb with tines about ⅛ in. (4 mm) apart

Yarn

Color	Yarn Brand	Weight of Yarn Ball	Qty.	No. of 3.5 oz. (100 g) Double Yarn Balls Needed	Actual Qty. Used
#911 NATURAL	DMC Merino Essential 4 Tweed	1.8 oz. (50 g)	2	1	3.5 oz. (100 g)
#8 SKY BLUE	Katia Merino Baby	1.8 oz. (50 g)	4	2	5.3 oz. (150 g)
BROWN (NOISETTE)	Phildar Charly	1.8 oz. (50 g)	2	1	0.4 oz. (10 g)
#766 GOLD	DMC Knitty 4	1.8 oz. (50 g)	2	1	0.5 oz. (15 g)
#20 DEEP ORANGE	Katia 100% Merino	1.8 oz. (50 g)	2	1	3.2 oz. (90 g)
#77 SALMON	Katia Merino Baby	1.8 oz. (50 g)	2	1	1.1 oz. (30 g) + 118 in. (300 cm)

F.Y.I.

Before embarking on this project, you should first have already tufted the Artemis Wall Hanging (pages 124 to 137).

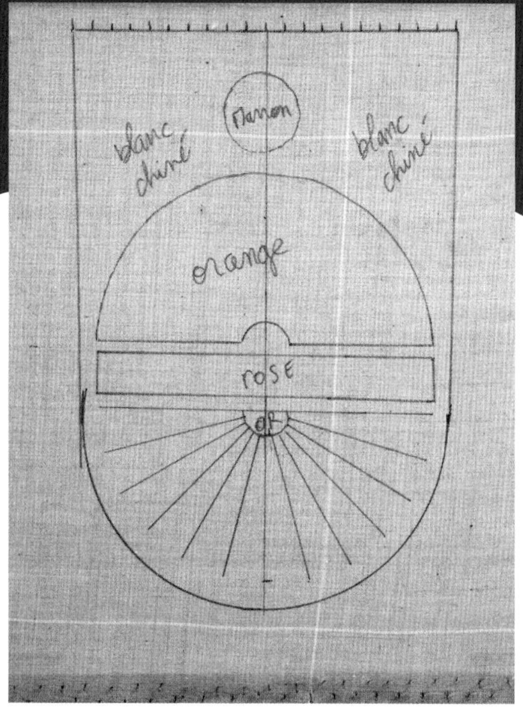

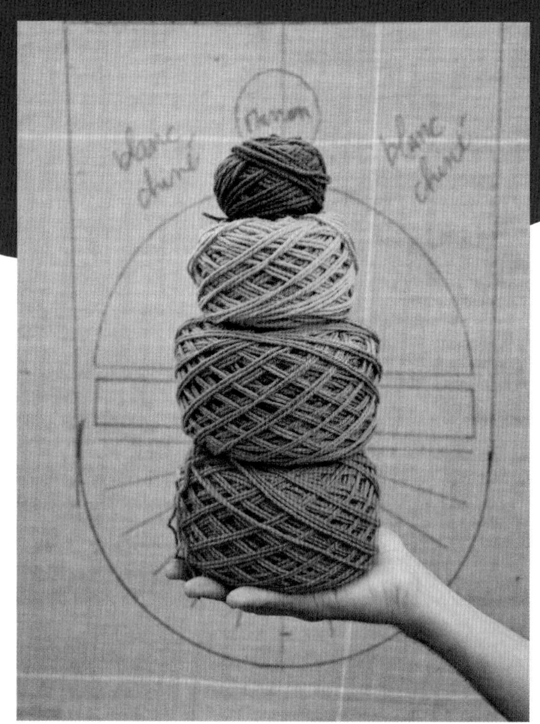

1 On the primary tufting cloth stretched over the frame, copy the 16 × 24 in. (40 × 60 cm) design with a marker and indicate the colors as well.

2 On the 16 in. (40 cm) side at the top, mark every 1 in. (2 cm) with a ruler (17 marks for 16 in. [21 marks for 40 cm]).

3 Make the double yarn balls needed per the table on page 139.

4 Tuft starting with the spokes, then work your way up. Fill in the shapes by drawing vertical lines (from bottom to top) side by side, leaving a very slight space between them.

5 On the back of the piece, remove any protruding strands by trimming them with regular or duckbill scissors, or by lightly pulling on them.

6 On the front side of the frame, trim and clean up the shapes using regular or duckbill scissors.

7 Tuft the outlines of the shapes and the edges of the wall hanging with the color white heather, then fill them in, always in vertical lines and from bottom to top. Remove any strands sticking out (see step 5).

8 Insert the salmon-colored yarn through the eye of the heavy-duty needle. You will need about 10 ft. (3 m) to make the loops around the dowel.

9 Follow steps 6 to 10 on pages 128 to 130.

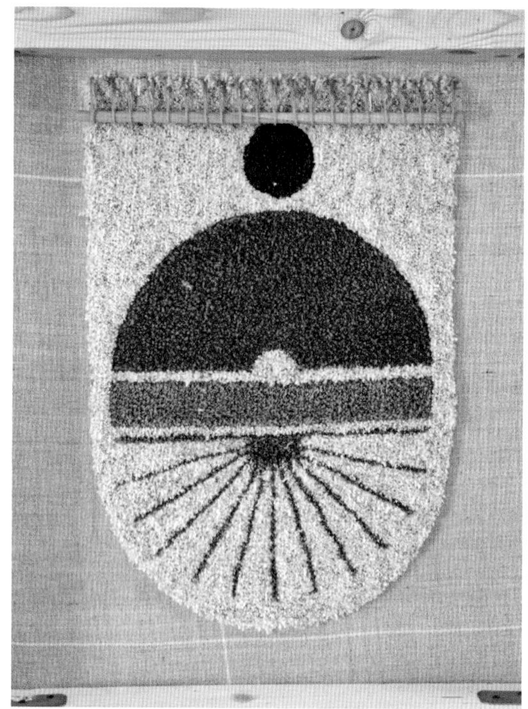

10 Place the dowel in the loops you just made. The piece should hang straight when hung up. Adjust the yarn so that the dowel is level and not tilted.

11 At the bottom of the design, draw two marks 2 in. (5 cm) apart.

12 Insert the strands of the double orange ball through the eye of the mattress needle.

13 Insert the needle into the first mark from the front and pull out about 16 ft. (5 m) of yarn.

14 Insert the needle from back to front at about ⅛ in. (2 mm) from the first mark and pull the yarn through.

15 Repeat this step until you reach the second mark, leaving loops of about 24 in. (60 cm) on the front of the wall hanging.

16 Take the two sky-blue double yarn balls and insert the four strands through the eye of the mattress needle.

17 As with the orange fringe, insert the needle into the tufting cloth (at the second spoke in the design) and pull out about 16 ft. (5 m) of yarn.

NOTE

You're going to spend a lot of time threading and pulling the needle through the fabric. Better to pull out 16 ft. (5 m) of yarn at a time to save time.

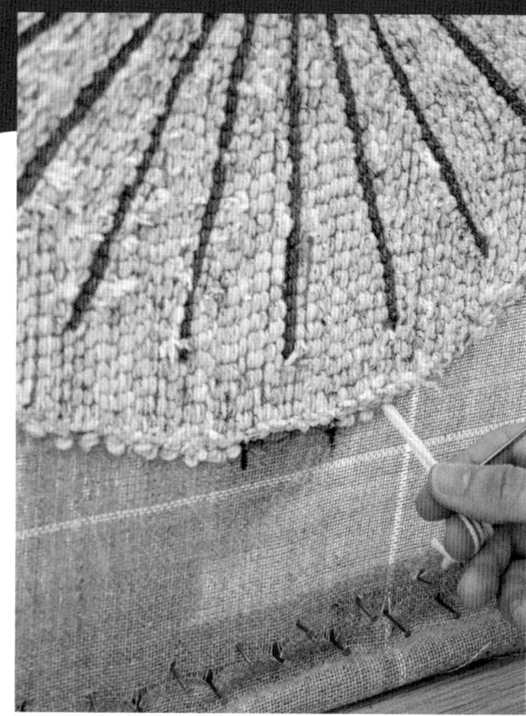

18 Insert the needle about 3⁄16 in. (5 mm) from the first hole and pull the yarn through—the spacing is larger than with the orange fringe, as there are four strands at the same time. Repeat this step, leaving loops of about 24 in. (60 cm) on the front of the wall hanging. When you run out of yarn, cut, and start again from step 16.

19 Continue until you reach the orange fringe, then cut the strands on the front side. Move to the other side of the orange and continue adding fringe.

20 For the gluing step, work vertically or horizontally, laying the frame down. Using a putty knife or disposable glove, coat the surface with carpet and flexible flooring adhesive, leaving a ½ in. (1.5 cm) border.

21 Using a trowel, apply the secondary fabric to the glue. Let dry for 12 hours.

22 Once the glue has dried, cut off the excess cloth with regular scissors, revealing the unglued edge.

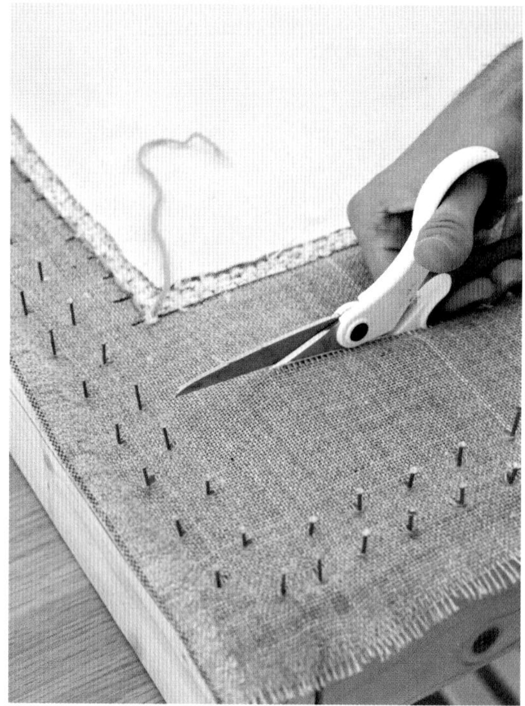

23 Again, using regular scissors, cut the primary cloth all around the piece, leaving a 2-in. (5-cm) border.

24 Check that the dowel is straight.

25 On the back of the piece, tie a knot at the ends of the pink yarn. Double it, if necessary (it needs to be large enough not to be pulled through to the other side). Trim excess yarn.

26 Cut the primary tufting cloth border down to ¾ in. (2 cm). Use the lighter trick to harden the cloth fibers (page 50).

27 Make notches every 2 in. (5 cm) along the curved edges of the wall hanging (this will make gluing easier).

28 To glue the finishing edges, follow steps 17 and 18 on pages 134 and 135, starting with the 16-in. (40-cm) side (with the 17-in. [42-cm] binding tape).

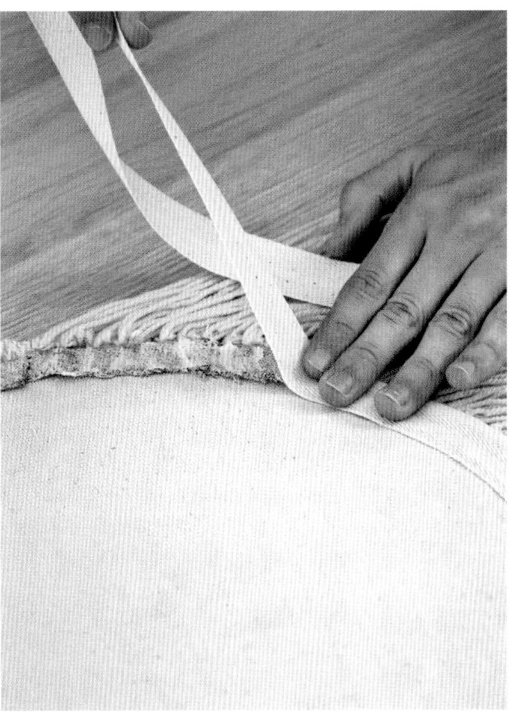

29 Then apply the 57-in. (145-cm) strip, taking the time to follow the curvature of the wall hanging.

30 When you have finished with the binding tape, let it dry for a few hours.

31 When the binding tape is dry, trim the ends using duckbill scissors.

32 Turn the piece over and brush with a wire brush.

33 Move on to shearing to smooth out the surface. Trim the shapes, if necessary.

34 Cut about 2 in. (5 cm) off the loops of light-blue fringe. Comb the fringe so the yarn strands are nice and straight.

.

35 Hang the wall hanging with a nail or screw. Little by little, trim the light-blue fringe to create a rounded shape. Each fringe should measure approximately 10 in. (25 cm).

36 Cut the orange fringe to a length of about 18 in. (45 cm).

Appendices

ONLINE RESOURCES

If you run into some problems while tufting, here is a list of sites that can help.

Tuft the World: **https://www.youtube.com/user/limescreen/videos**

Tufting Love: **tuftipedia.com**

Various YouTube channels are dedicated to this craft: **Tuft the World**, **Tuftinglove** and **Tuftingshop**.

GLOSSARY

C

carpet carving clippers. Tool for shearing the yarn to smooth the carpet.

carpet grippers. Wooden strips with nails to be placed on a frame to hold the primary backing.

clamps. Tools to attach the frame securely to a table.

cotton herringbone tape. Strips used around the edges for finishing a project.

cut-pile. Action of a tufting gun which cuts wool at high speed for a tufted finish.

D

duckbill scissors or applique scissors. Scissors for cutting small details.

F

frame. Wooden frame for hanging the primary backing to be tufted.

L

loop-pile. Action of a tufting gun that creates loops through the canvas without cutting the wool.

N

needle threader. Tool for passing yarn through the tufting gun more easily.

S

secondary backing cloth. Fabric used (cotton, felt, etc.) for the back of the rug.

T

tuft/tufting. Technique for inserting yarn onto a canvas at high speed using a tufting gun.

tufting cloth. Main fabric of the tufting, composed most often of cotton and polyester.

tufting gun. Main working tool of tufting. It is an electric machine that inserts yarn at high speed onto a stretched canvas.

Y

yarn. Main material used for tufting. Wool yarn is most often used, but other types of yarn can also be tufted.

yarn winder. Hand-cranked machine for making balls of yarn.

ACKNOWLEDGMENTS

I'd like to extend my warmest thanks to all the people who have been on this wonderful adventure with me from the outset: my darling mom, Yasmine, Marine, Alima, Mathilde, Kévin, Jean-Baptiste, Clément, Florence, my brother Steeve, and my dad, who would have been very proud of this book.

Many thanks to Anne-Lise for supporting me during the writing of this book and to Éditions Eyrolles for their trust in me. Thanks to Sabine for her photos and cheerfulness, to Karima for her valuable assistance, to the Domestika France team, and to all those who follow me on social media in this crazy adventure!

ABOUT THE AUTHOR

After a career in communication and fashion, **Guillaume Neves** became passionate about textile arts. Disappointed not to find the carpet of his dreams, he tried tufting and fell in love with the technique. Under his brand Atelier Paolo, he creates rugs and other tufted creations with sunny designs and vibrant colors. He teaches tufting to others in his workshop in Bordeaux and on the online creative course platform Domestika.